Issue No. 3

Published by Eastern Heroes Publishing
Produced by Rick Baker
Additional material and images: Toby Russell
Editor: Rick Baker
Design, production & layout: Nick Cairns,
22:22 Creative Media
Cover art: Shaolin Jaa, Crike99Art

Printing: Ingramspark

IngramSpark

CONTRIBUTORS:

UK
Toby Russell, Tim Hollingworth, Paul Dre,
Michael Nesbitt, Ken Miller, Alan Donkin,
Simon Pritchard, Martin Sandison, Ron
London Ivey, Steven Morris, Johnny Burnett,
Scott Adkins, Ron Ivey, Ben Johnson

Germany
Thorston Boose

USA
Michael Worth, Jason McNeil, Andy Smith,
Hector Martinez , Andrew P Bovell

Hong Kong
Mike Leeder, Chong Siew-lam

Special Thanks to
Bruce li, Scott Adkins, James Bennett, Loren
Avedon, Lee A Charles, Mark Strange,
Jackie Chan, Al Leong, Soo Cole – Fighting
Spirit Film Festival, Hye-Jung Jeon – London
East Asian Film Festival

For advertising rates contact
Easternheroesshop@gmx.co.uk

Editor

It seems that Eastern Heroes [is]
going from strength to strength and growing
in size!

The original page count for issue one was not to
exceed seventy-two pages, it went over by some
ten pages. Issue No. 2 was to not exceed eighty-
four pages; it ended up at 100 pages. So! I said,
"Please let this issue stay within 100 pages." As you can see, it's gone way over
that magic number. Being the editor I try to reign it in the best I can, but I get so
many good articles submitted that I just say "Let's go with it".

So! For issue No. 3, the only item I have cut out is my own Rick's Round-Up.
God knows what issue No. 4 page count will be.

The most important thing is to acknowledge the contributors, the talented
people that do the design layout and the stunning covers that have been created
by Shaolin Jaa and Crike@99art these really are the backbone of the magazine's
success. But I did add my two-pennyworth this issue, by creating the Sparta
section and interviewing and giving praise to five hardworking guys that help keep
this industry ticking.

So welcome to another fully-loaded issue covering enough subjects to satisfy
action fans of all genres. As always, thank you so much for supporting Eastern
Heroes magazine and in those immortal words…

Keep the faith   *Rick Baker*   Rick Baker

Contents

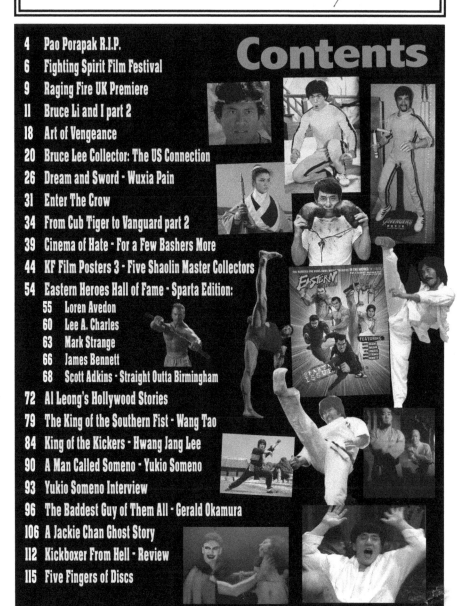

PAO PORAPAK R.I.P.
เป้า ปรปักษ์

by Toby Russell

"PAO PORAPAK" or real name Winai Yuenyong, director and famous supporting actor, on October 17, 2019 died peacefully at the age of 71 after a long battle with cancer.

Pao Porapak often played ruffian roles such as hitmen, drug dealers, psychos and knifemen. He won three Thai cinema awards. He was stuntman, actor, stunt director and director.

I tell people "If Panna Rittikrai is the Thai Jackie then Pao Porapak is the Thai Sammo Hung".

During the '80s Pao was part of the Sorapong Group, making about a dozen films with Soropong; titles like; *Deadline*, *Marvelous Tale*, *Who Killed My Brother*, *Ninja Fantasy* and *Wolf*. Later, in the '80s and '90s, he also appeared in some Panna Rittikrai productions such as *The Black Goblins*.

In the mid to late '90s he went into TV, mainly choreography, some directing too, but there was never much business in that field and the action films sort of died out.

Following that he went to live with the Hmong Hill tribe people near Chang Mai and made some excellent action films with the tribe, but those films are very hard to find.

In the later years of his life Pao found it increasingly difficult to support himself due to the dwindling Thai action movie and TV industry. He ended up living out of his car until he became terminally ill with cancer.

A sad end to a brilliant career that all started with Bruce Lee's *Big Boss*, where a young Pao played one of the exploited ice factory workers.

PAO PORAPAK (HIGHLIGHTED) IN BIG BOSS

FIGHTING SPIRIT Film Festival

by Ron Ivey

I like to keep my articles short and sweet for an easy read, but how do I cram so much into a few paragraphs? I'll give it a go...

"We aim to support, connect, recognise, inspire, and promote martial arts and action through film." – Soo Cole

I met Soo Cole (the founder of FSFF) at the SENI Combat and Strength Show 2014, held that year in the London Soccer Dome. Soo was there with some Shaolin monks who were doing a display, and I was there for the Eastern Heroes Hwang Jang-lee event. I then met Soo again at the East Winds Film Festival, held at Coventry University, it was great to meet someone like myself, regularly going to, and supporting events! Also, myself and several friends visited the the Shaolin Temple UK, where Soo was kind enough to show us around.

Soo had spoken to me when the idea for a film festival was first forming. And with a lot of passion and enthusiasm Soo pushed onwards until the festival was a reality. With help from Paul of SENI who was putting on an event, the Fighting Spirit Film Festival arrived as part of the SENI Combat and Strength Show 2016.

The first Fighting Spirit Film Festival was a one day event in the Cineworld cinema within London's Millennium Dome, which would lead to an event (or two) every year onwards. A selection of cinemas have been used across London, the film festival has now found a home at Stratford Picturehouse, and most of the events have been held there.

Eastern Heroes was also at SENI in 2016 for both days, with special guest Hwang In-shik. Fighting Spirit Film Festival went under the radar for many, partly due to its location and it being an unknown quantity at that time. I had posted about it beforehand in my Facebook events group, but it takes a lot to get some people to an event. I walked several people up from Eastern Heroes which was based in the Water Margin (bar/restaurant) to Fighting Spirit in Cineworld. Some of us watched the martial arts displays, short films, and a few watched *Drunken Master*, and bought merchandise from Andrew Stanton.

Soo's team of volunteers has grown over the years and deserves a shout-out: Weng, Es, Clayre, William, Tim and many more. FSFF2021 also had Jessa, Elara, Curtis, Kirk, Eli, IJ, Matt, Dario, Charles and myself. A loyal team, with a lot of knowledge and skill sets between them.

There is a focus on helping creative talent, Soo has given short film makers a chance to see their work at a cinema! There are hours of short films, with a mix of stories but all contain the same theme, martial arts.

I have been part of the team on several occasions, Soo has a solid, reliable team working behind the scenes. But it is Soo that is the driving force that created, and pushes FSFF forward, without Soo there would be no FSFF and that would be a sad day for all aspiring martial art film makers, as this could be the only chance for them to see their work at the cinema.

Through passion, not greed, I have seen FSFF grow. Through generosity, not selfish self-promotion FSFF continues to survive and support. It is truly refreshing to see an event promoting others!

There have been many martial arts demonstrations at FSFF, from various clubs, karate to wushu and everything in between.

As well as the London events, there have been screenings in Birmingham at the Mockingbird Cinema.

Fighting Spirit Birmingham 2019 hosted the UK Premiere of *Master Z*, and *Triple Threat*. Scott Adkins also did a Q&A after the screening of *Triple Threat*.

Scott Adkins has been a fantastic patron of the FSFF and has helped to sell out screenings and bring the festival to a wider audience, also attending premiere screenings of *Accident Man*, *Debt Collector*, and *Ip Man 4*.

I have shone a light on Soo's festival from the beginning, and more people are attending a Fighting Spirit screening every year. I look forward to its continued growth, and potential collaborations.

At every London FSFF event I've attended, either working, or as a paying customer, I have enjoyed some superb days out. The FSFF team also collaborated with Mike Fury for the awesome *Avengement* premiere screening, which for many was the event of that year with almost every cast member in attendance.

2021 has seen another mix of feature films, shorts and a documentary on Pat Morita. There was a surprise message from Cynthia Rothrock talking about FSFF2021 and the short films which Cynthia is also a judge of, it was nice for all her fans to see this message on the big screen and to hint at a potential visit to London's FSFF2022. *Paper Tigers* was premiered, and is one of the better examples of what martial artists and creative talent can put together with a small budget, and was a film well suited to the FSFF.

"Sadly two of the Fighting Spirit family passed away, and it was important to pay tribute to Max Repossi and Steven Booth, who both made significant contributions to the Fighting Spirit Film Festival. Steven Booth was a great sounding board when FSFF was still being developed as an idea, and believed in it from the get go. Max first came to FSFF in 2018 when we first held the event at Stratford Picturehouse and he not only had a film in the short film competition, he also performed martial arts demonstrations that year and again in 2019. Both of them with their energy, enthusiasm and support, along with the many people who have attended have helped make FSFF what it is."
— Soo Cole

Eastern Heroes had a merchandise table again this year, selling their latest magazines, posters and books. Rick and Simon also had a selection of framed posters on display, as well as other contributions from Shaolin Jaa, Crike99Art and Mouine Omari, and these were spread around the venue.

FSFF2021 wrapped up with a screening of *Armour Of God*. FSFF have screened many classics, including *36th Chamber of Shaolin* and *Dragons Forever*, to name a few, the classic film screening is very much a part of every FSFF. Matt Routledge had commented that the last screening of *Armour Of God* he was aware of was in 1993 at the Prince Charles Cinema! FSFF gives fans another chance to see these films on the big screen amongst fellow fans.

Armour Of God was introduced by film director Matt Routledge, with a mention of the recent sad loss of Brad Allan, Matt told a great anecdote about seeing Brad scaling a building as Jackie Chan walked by! Before the film, a framed *Armour Of God* poster donated to FSFF by Simon Gardner of Asian Movie Posters and Rick Baker

of Eastern Heroes was raffled, with the money raised split between both the families of Stephen and Max.

If you like martial arts, films, and a day with a good vibe, then give FSFF a try. You can follow the Fighting Spirit Film Festival on social media for the latest news.

FSFF2021 team photo courtesy of Curtis Harvey from *Combat* and *Strength Magazine*. Thanks also go to the Stratford Picturehouse team.

Wishing Soo and the team, many more successful events.
https://www.fightingspiritfilmfestival.com
See you out there…

RAGING FIRE
UK Premiere
at the London East Asia Film Festival

by Ron Ivey

"The return to cinemas has been a long arduous journey. The last eighteen months have seen cinemas close and audiences have turned to their small screens for entertainment. But the collective tradition is far from dead. Films have and will hopefully always be made to be shown in the cinema, in the company of others."
— LEAFF Festival Director HYEJUNG JEON

Raging Fire was enjoyed even more, for having been screened at a lively film festival. No film review needed, just some photos of a top night out at the London East Asia Film Festival's opening film.

The sixth year of LEAFF opened with a bang, well, more of a crash, bang, wallop as *Raging Fire* exploded onto the screen!

"The streets of Hong Kong once again explode with action in this high-octane chase thriller, the final film by one of the masters of the genre, Benny Chan".

Call Of Heroes was my last lads day out to a Benny Chan film. This time around it was a get-together with fellow East Asia film fans at LEAFF 2021. The film is always a small part of a top night out, good food and great company boost any film to another level on the big screen, especially at a fantastic cinema in the luxury electric reclining stall seats.

After eating in London's Soho with Eastern Heroes' Rick Baker and friends, it was off to Leicester Square. There was a queue outside the Odeon Lux, and as we walked in it was obvious it would be a very busy night.

There was a separate V.I.P.

area upstairs, which we visited to mingle with a mixed crowd of journalists from several newspapers, sponsors and those that are known on the East Asia event scene.

We then moved outside the V.I.P. area to chat to the film fans, who are the backbone of any event, it is us that buy tickets and attend these events that support the scene. We then made our way to the stalls seating and found our LEAFF tote bags filled with food, Soju and literature on the seats. Always quality and attention to detail from the LEAFF team. Before the film, amongst others there was a speech by Festival Director Hye-jung Jeon and a greeting by Gilford

Law the Director-General of the Hong Kong Economic and Trade Office.

The film's action played out well on the big screen, and it was a great final film from Benny Chan. "It's a set-up that will please fans of the golden age of heroic bloodshed movies, when John Woo, Ringo Lam, Johnnie To and Tsui Hark transformed Hong Kong into a battleground between gangsters and the law."

This is an action film best suited to a cinema visit, catch it if you can. Trinity Cine Asia will be releasing *Raging Fire* from 12th November 2021 in the UK, the film will also be released on Blu-Ray, DVD, and Digital on the 10th of January 2022.

Another Benny Chan film screened at this festival was *A Moment Of Romance* (1990), starring Andy Lau.

There were far too many films and documentaries for me to list individually, but there was something for everyone at this year's London East Asia Film Festival.

There was even a 'Taste of Asia' menu in collaboration with Michelin-starred Head Chef Joo Won. This was available at two venues, offering a range of tantalising dishes.

Also, a Zoom seminar called Screen to Screen, took place where participants were encouraged to present questions to LEAFF's esteemed panel of festival experts.

I attended this year's festival several times, and on each occasion I noticed a high level of professionalism from everyone involved. Each venue was chosen with care, with quality screenings and attention to detail throughout.

I went to two screenings at The Cinema At Selfridges, and once again LEAFF managed to add a fresh fun location to their list of venues used to screen a film.

The closing Gala's Halloween sold out screening of *Spiritwalker* was a surprise hit with plenty of gunplay and several well choreographed fight scenes. The Halloween party after *Spiritwalker* was a lovely way to end yet another imaginative film festival.

A special thank you and congratulations to the London East Asia Film Festival team, for this fantastic film festival which was thoroughly enjoyed by everyone that went.

LEAFF 2021 showcased three International, five European and eighteen UK premieres with features from China, Hong Kong, Japan, Korea, the Philippines, Taiwan, Thailand and Vietnam.

I am told planning for early 2022 screenings are already underway. See you out there…

BRUCE LI & I

Part 2

by Michael Worth

何宗道

If one were to sum up the idea of who Bruce Li is to the genre of kung fu cinema, it would go something like this: he was a Bruce Lee imitator. Widespread as that supposition can be, the truth of the man runs much much deeper and in some ways, antithetical to that assumption. Li, or Ho Tsung Tao, in many ways was a talented young dreamer who aspired to bring both his acting and martial arts training to the big screen. As a high school student exposed to Lee on the big screen in *Fist of Fury* (Lo Wei, 1972 – *The Big Boss* was released afterwards in Taiwan) he was instantly inspired ("Wow!", he declared. "What kind of kung fu is this? This is real kung fu!!"), but his goals lay well outside of the legend of his inspiration, even if his destiny had other ideas.

THE NEW MARTIAL ARTS MASTER...
BRUCE LI

"If you look back at your accomplishments, do you remember anything specifically memorable as an actor?"

"Yes, like I've always felt that I wasn't able to portray him, Bruce Lee, 100%"
— Bruce Li

THE CHINATOWN KID

The eighteen unit luxury apartment building now called The Palace that rests on the corner of Powell Avenue in San Francisco formerly housed a gateway to a mystifying universe of martial arts for the western world. This once-titled Pagoda Palace Theater (converted to a Chinese language movie theater in 1967 from an old vaudeville theater) was my education in the cinematic art that exists within the Chinese kung fu

films. Though hardly reasonable grounds for a shift of consciousness, my young brain registered these films in a wholly new way once I had viewed them in the original language for the first time with fancy foreign film subtitles. It was where I began to stand up and take notice of the camera work and the choreography, no longer distracted by the over the top dubbing. Seated among a crowd who most likely did not require the translations, I was beginning to take notice of the artistry that existed in the matinee mayhem and how a history of collective talent had built this thing we called Kung Fu Movies.

BRUCE LI THE INVINCIBLE

"Why wasn't Taiwan's movie industry successful, because it was mostly about love stories. Oh flower, oh you love me, I love you. Just walking. No fighting."

As I crossed the grass, Ho Tsung-tao was holding a weathered pair of focus mitts on his hands for a father and son who were wrapping up a training session with him at the far end of a park. In this southern edge of Taiwan, the sun was falling low in the horizon, the heat and humidity settling into a relaxing breeze. The father/son clones were separated by a generation not just of age but of influence and culture. The older one was now exposing his child to a man who had inspired him as a younger man, explaining this once industry-goaded action star had now found the kind of peace his characters in movies were frequently fighting for.

Ho looked over at me and laughed after his training session, touched his chest as he took in some breaths: "When I was young, I was a tiger. Strong tiger. But now I am a weak cat because I'm old." I laughed with him but can tell you as he turned I noted his forearms were notably shaped like clubs, his legs though stiffening from the exertion, distinctly sturdy. He was not the fresh faced avenger from *Fist of Fury Part 2*, but he still exhibited his years of experience within both his frame and his persona.

"Have you ever watched a movie called *Silence of the Lambs*?", he asked us as he began to get settled on a cement slab in the center of the park. "The murderer had a needle with him, and he uses that needle to end their victims life by pushing it into their necks and they would die without any suffer. He sees it as ending their lives

One of the first films I attended there was titled *Blind Fist of Bruce* (Luk Bong, 1979). The recent recognition of a comic fighter named Jackie Chan and the new martial comedy films were offering up to the west a plethora of new styled action features such as *The Fearless Hyena* (Jackie Chan, 1979) and *World of Drunken Master* (Joseph Kuo, 1979), but it was not often that this new sub-genre would include the addition of the well-known Bruce Lee 'tribute artist': Bruce Li. I was already underlining the TV guide for the unpredictable airings of *Dynamo* (Hua Shan, 1978) or *Bruce Li The Invincible* (Law Kei, 1978) so Li was already on my radar, yet this would be the first time I

had taken notice of the artist behind the martial. This was no *Citizen Kane*, but Li in an uncharacteristic vulnerability, was expressing a faulty and imperfect human being on a road to the consummate, in a way I had not yet seen up on that Chinatown movie screen. Many years later he would tell me; "What is important is within the person, him or herself, with their emotion that they convey through their eyes." I may not have relied on Bruce Li as I would a Steve Mcqueen or Brando for my acting education, but his presence in my childhood would inform me how the artist should always lift up the art, not the other way around.

FIST OF THE TOAD

BEHIND BRUCE LEE

before the disease spreads. I wanted to film that mentality. A mentality, which is a shame that I didn't get a chance, of a better performance." Ho, in settling down to recall his career as an actor, had immediately begun shaking his head, as if the memories were something he hadn't grappled with in a long time. It was as if he was about to enter into a retention where he had not traveled in years. One particular thought purging first: "Let me tell you, the director of *The Green Hornet* (*Bruce Against the Supermen*, Wu Chia-chun 1975) … I don't know what he was doing".

As an actor/filmmaker, I can attest to his nagging and haunting feelings of regret or perfection when it comes to your work. The aspiration to achieve greatness is rarely achieved even by great talents, whose nature is cruelly to always strive for more than they are capable of. There is rarely even 'good enough'. Our creative minds tend to be several steps ahead of our own abilities often leaving even our best efforts unexceptional in our minds. With what I could only describe as a ruefulness, he seemed to look at me as if to say; "You guys really want to hear about this crazy ride?"

STORY OF THE DRAGON

"Last time (someone wanted to talk) about my life, they were gathering research on how many movies I've starred in," he let me know. "I shot thirty of them. But they found more than seventy!" When I followed up trying to understand how that can be,, he began to relay a story of working on *Story of the Dragon* (William Cheung Kei, 1976) for producer William Lan Tin-hung, In which scenes were filmed with a zoom lens and then re-filmed on the same lens but in a different focal size (ie: closer or wider) and then those variations were ultimately used in other productions. After his recounting, he laughed. "But I was only paid for one."

Story of the Dragon for me as a teen was the ugly step child of *Bruce Lee The Man The Myth*. It had its odd charm and unique Lee-isms (the Wing Chun school sequences contain several modified lessons from Bruce Lee's JKD playbook) but fell short of the more attested qualities of the Ng See-yuen production. Right in line with Ho's recollection of the film, *Story*'s western release title was *Bruce Lee's Deadly Kung Fu* (or *Bruce Lee's Secret*), though companies like L&T Films – who were notorious for retitling previously released films with unique one-off titles of their own – also dubbed this pseudo Bruce Lee bio-pic *The Dragon's Life*. The poster proclaimed, "Bruce Lee ran his San Francisco school of kung fu and lived a true story of daring adventure." It began to dawn on me as I explained to him in the production company's defense, that these

dissociative title disorders could possibly have caused the rapid title increase within his resume. He shrugged, "Even I can get confused."

BECOMING A DYNAMO

"I never thought too highly of my skills. I always think that I'm not good enough."

Ho's many incarnations on screen are how any of us ever knew him, his alter-egos, his imaginary beings. But who was the man before he took those first movie punches, before an army of kung fu fans would discover him in theaters?? Turns out like the rest of us, he was a youth who discovered his divine guidance through the movie screen. "Life is short! You don't get to accomplish much in a lifetime. You can be a student, a kid, you can get married, be a dad…but in movies, you can live in the old times, you can live in the modern day, in the future! Anything is possible!" Ho's background was the ideal for an artist; once rich in youth followed soon by a painful hardship. His father, a wealthy business man, lost it all during the 'Japanese era' forcing Ho through multiple schools and home changes. Ho's interest in film began early but was he was initially unable to, "So I ended up studying Physical Education. Sport was my hobby. I enjoyed doing gymnastic and boxing with my classmates".

Later, after graduation, Ho started his next education in the Taiwan Film Institute with fellow classmates Dick Wei (*The Five Venoms*,1978) and future Bruceploitation

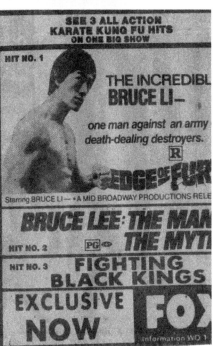

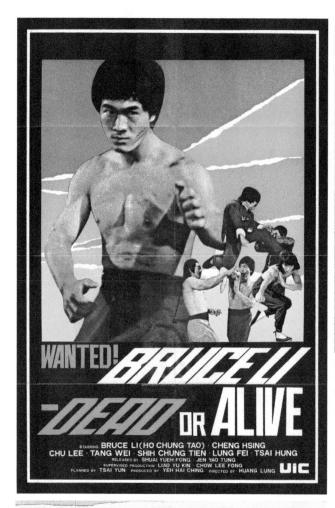

BEFORE
FISTS OF FURY
AND
ENTER THE DRAGON
BRUCE LEE RAN HIS
SAN FRANCISCO
SCHOOL OF KUNG FU
AND LIVED A
TRUE STORY OF
DARING ADVENTURE.

Now-a true story from the early days of Bruce Lee... learn how the Dragon got his name and discover...

THE DRAGON'S LIFE

R RESTRICTED

EXPRESS THE UTMOST WITH THE MINIMUM

L&T FILMS CORPORATION LTD. PRESENT

world he was thrust into, many even more successful talents around him would not reflect the same core dedication that Ho sought. This is not some fan boy hyperbole. The more I got to know him, the more his utter perfectionism and creative artistry showed through his persona. "I was attentive. On film sets," he noted. "I helped the cameraman to hold his camera(s). I was the lead, but I helped him. Why? I was working out my muscle!" I was fully aware of what that creative 'muscle' meant, expanding the skill set and knowledge within a field you were blessed to be in. Since first stepping on the cement of Hollywood Blvd. I have studied the many arts that make up filmmaking because it was important for me to survive or fall knowing my skill sets. Ho did not stroll through his production jobs or survive off his good fortune either, he was a student of his chosen art.

As a ten year old I bought with my allowance (and a little help from mom) my first two Super 8mm cameras, writing, shooting and editing my own mini features including *Fists of the Toad* (Michael Worth, 1981) a Bruceploitation film set in Berkeley, California. Ho as it turns out was no less inspired as he began his career; "I did buy two 8mm cameras. I made two movies. One in Taiwan, one in Hong Kong. I filmed and edited myself. All by myself just for fun. A passion of mine." Ho's increasing interest in camera work ("I learned that by myself. Observing the cameramen mostly."), would

actor Lung Tien-hsiang (*The True Game of Death*, 1979) where "I was the best behaved student in my class. I sat in the very front. We learned about make up, directing, shooting, props... I took notes in details. I treated everything seriously. Not everyone did." This for my mind would reflect his future career as well. Though Ho's ability and dedication would often be mired in the exploitation

lead not just to a better filmmaking acumen but several turns at the director's chair with *Fists of Bruce Lee* and *Counter Attack* (1979, 1981). As mentioned, Li has suffered at the hands of both mainstream kung fu fans and Bruce Lee admirers as a second-rate action actor, but as I was learning, my youthful hero-worship of him was not for naught.

After Ho graduated from his training he appeared in several films as an extra or stuntman and even a lion dancer in one production. But it would be *Gecko Kung Fu* (Wong Ho, 1972) that Li considered his first real acting role taking on the transitional villain role. He was also discovering that education and the real-world did not always comport, the often varying working techniques of directors and actors forcing Ho to continue adapting to the needs of camera. But he was also one to not lose sight of breaking the mold, and it was Bruce Lee that served as illustration of that. "The good guys are supposed to look straight," explaining the traditional screen acting techniques. "You don't do sidelong glances. Bruce Lee was always doing sidelong glances! See, every actor is different." Caryn Stedman who portrayed Linda Lee with Ho in *He's a Legend, He's a Hero* (Wong Sing-loy, 1976) commented to me on this later: "The direction was very interesting because sometimes I got the feeling that we were being directed for stage acting rather than film acting. Because you know, when you act on stage, and I had done some stage acting before, your gestures are much larger." Many assume Ho was inspired by Lee simply to emulate him but as it was turning out, this motivation was directed towards his own evaluation. He was not concerned about mimicking Lee's 'sidelong glance', it was the concept "that every actor is different".

Ho's early work in Taiwan was a studio system procedure, one which an of actor today who joins a traditional production with a very specific script and schedule may not well understand. Ho would not always know what movie he was working on that day. He was picked up by a rental bus with other actors and taken to the studio where they would shoot. He would occasionally drive himself but noted: "If we were hitting many locations, then it's actually more convenient to get the ride from work." Li's principle at the institute was a man named Joseph Kong (*The Clones of Bruce Lee*, 1980) who himself would go on to direct a volume of Ho's Bruceploitation brethren Bruce Le's films. Ho would work for a while as an intern for Kong's production company in these early years "But I never actually worked directly for him." It would be in 1973 when Bruce Lee passed away that the tide would begin to quickly turn for Ho. "Unbelievable! He was like a god." Ho shook his head, seeming to convey that disbelief that many still do almost fifty years later. "He was invincible. How on earth could he die? I didn't believe it." Later that day I would offer him a few English magazines on Bruce Lee I had

NOW THE KING OF KUNG-FU COMES BACK TO LIFE!

THE BRUCE LEE STORY

HOW HE LIVED!
HOW HE LOVED!
HOW HE FOUGHT!
HOW HE DIED!

ALL NEW!

SEE the truth explode in...

The DRAGON DIES HARD

- A HALLMARK Presentation -   COLOR   R

brought with me. I watched as he flipped through the pages, staring gratefully at the images his head once again shaking, the feeling clear: "what a shame".

At the end of 1974, Ho joined the army. "I served for two years then came back and made more movies." One of Ho's returning films within the Bruce Lee biographical entries was *He's a Legend, He's a Hero* (released in the U.S. as *The Dragon Lives*)

filmed in Taiwan. I had seen this film several years later in San Francisco on a double bill with an *Exorcist* rip-off titled *Night Child* (1976), and what I had found interesting about the movie was its take on Lee's demise via his obsession with physical excellence. But not just any ol' gym fanatic, his 'demon' of choice was an American made training device he kept in his home. This monster of a machine looked more like the Prince of Darkness than a Lat Pull Down Device. Caryn White, a model living in Taiwan at the time, found herself offered the role of Lee's wife in the film after an Australian martial artist friend working on the production helped her meet director Wong for extra work. "In the film, there's a lot of the psychological drama, which kind of surprised me, I didn't expect them to do all that. But they know that whole dark scene where he's in the studio, he's in his his training room, and he won't come out. And I was really surprised that they went into that because that, you know, that was moving into more of kind of the psychological aspect of Bruce Lee." Unlike *Bruce Lee The Man The Myth* (Ng See-yuen, 1976) or even *Bruce Lee Super Dragon* (Lin Bing, 1976) where Lee's death was rarely focused on with such fault or intensity, Legend seemed to be exploring it prominently for an answer.

Caryn also noted, "I think they were kind of making up the stories as they are going along. They did have some skeletal biography of Bruce Lee, a highly fictional biography of Bruce Lee, but they did have some things about his life that were absolutely true in the film." On this matter, Ho was also very aware of the historically loose productions. "Lots of them [the productions] did not have scripts. It became kind of chaotic. Sometimes they wrote a few pages on the set, 'Hey, these are today's lines.' they'd tell us. Yah, but what was the scene? The lines were whatever." Though Ho still found merit within the unorthodox production, claiming Sing-Loy was a 'great' director, helping Ho discover how important it was to act with his eyes, "He said that if I weren't able to tell the stories with my eyes, everything else would be worthless."

I can tell you in my years of knowing him that his interest in discussing acting as much as martial arts is clear. His love of filmmaking and the craft behind it was at the forefront of his pursuit and hearing him discuss it, I could not help but once again identify how Ho swimming in a sea of exploitation and rushed productions left a legacy of cinema that still has new fans coming to his films.

Our crew left after a few hours as we had to make our way back to Tai Pei on one of the evening trains. I finished the day up getting a dozen of my poster collection from childhood signed by the man they pivoted around. For once in my life, I turned into an autograph hound and was not going to deny it. Over the next few days we spent the final whirlwind of meetings with people like Dragon Lee, David Chiang and the late Roy Horan. But Ho Tsung Tao and the man who he had become would not leave my mind. I planned another trip for the following year, but this time I had requested some training time with him. Ho kindly obliged and almost a year to the day later I arrived to Taiwan again with my friend Frank Djeng, former Marketing Manager for Tai Seng Video, and brought my camera gear to work on my own documentary project. We met at the park once more and he came prepared; focus mitts, air shield, boxing gloves and Kali sticks. Ho had spent some time with Dan Inosanto on the film *The Chinese Stuntman* (Bruce Li, 1981). "I wanted to talk about Jeet Kune Do (in that film)," he pointed out. "There was the egg scene, the sandbag scene… used to show the force and the method used in JKD. That's why I hired Dan Inosanto." Inosanto was also one of the very first instructors I sought in my arrival in Los Angeles where I studied at his Academy in Marina Del Rey, so Ho and I began warming up by sharing our personal interchanges with him while practicing with the Kali sticks. It is hard to communicate that moment with proper effect but with each clash of the wooden sticks, staring into the face of the man who I had seen defeat Lo Lieh, Bolo and Phillip Ko Fei on screen dozens of times… Well, phantasmagoric scarcely conveys it.

Ho's first film for a Hong Kong based production would be a big one; *Bruce Lee True Story* or *Bruce Lee The Man, The Myth* (Ng See-yuen, 1976). "[*The Man The Myth*] was a success," Ho explained as we took a break and I brought up one of my favorite films of his. "Some people told me to raise my price, I told them no. I just want to make good movies. I actually cut my price in half for [*The Man, The Myth*]. Why? Because I wanted to show people how Bruce Lee's real kung fu was all about." I was reminded again that Ho's genuine attempt to honour Lee and his teaching rather than simply simulate it was always at his core. I let him know that many consider the film if not wholly accurate the most instructive of both 'the

myths and the man' than any other bio-pic. The film would expand Ho's popularity and presence in Hong Kong and begin a new leg of productions. During shooting he had dinner with Yuen Woo-ping who was discussing a new film he was planning to make with Ng See-yuen called *Snake in the Eagle's Shadow* (Yuen Woo Ping, 1978). "See, Yuen was already prepping for *Snake in the Eagle's Shadow*," Ho said. "He (Yuen Woo-ping) was going to be the director. I knew (Jackie Chan) was gonna be very successful with this."

Jackie Chan and Ho Tsung Tao had

recently overlapped their careers with dueling productions that both intended to follow up the legend of Bruce Lee's Chen Chen in *Fist of Fury*. Director Lee Tso-nam had half of the original cast (Tien Feng, etc) for *Fist of Fury Part 2* starring Ho while Lo Wei had the other (Nora Miao, etc) for his version, *New Fist of Fury* (Lo Wei, 1976) with Chan. This timely production clash was not unnoticed by anyone at the time, they were "competing with each other. Mine did better," he said with a laugh. I mentioned that Tarantino had liked his film more than the original and even screened it every so often in Los Angeles. Ho smiled again (as he was prone to do), calling him "that wild director," but humbly disagreeing, "Bruce Lee was special." But so is Ho, as he was often in Lee Tso-nam's hands, turning maybe less than special work into something memorable. *Fury Part 2* would always rest securely in the top group of 'Must have Bruce Li films.' There is a tone or quality that can exists within a film to make it memorable that even the artists who made it can not always explain. Lee Tso-nam had told me specifically about making *Fury Part 2*: "We try to watch the original film again, find out its strength, then when we shoot the sequel, or the remake, we can put in something in it didn't have (before), then we follow the main plot, but also try to be as different as possible." My first viewing of it at The Warfield Theater on Market Street had immediately left an impression; it was on a double bill with *Bruce and The Iron Finger* (To Man-bo, 1979) which Ho also recalled. "We worked in Taiwan," he remembered. "Bruce Leung Siu-lung, Sham Chin-bo – we called him Lil Bo, and a group of lion dancers from Hong Kong. Bruce Leung Siu-lung was kind and easygoing".

Ho had to open his clinic that was several blocks away so we grabbed up our equipment and made the short trek across the narrow cobblestone streets. The small, slender office was already open, a few of his patients waiting inside. Ho offered us a piece of chocolate from his desk while professing the health benefits of eating "70% and above cocoa" content. I was not one to argue as watching his energy and focus it was clear he was doing something right. I began to watch him at work, with the community that was now flowing in and out of his office. Seeing the man I had watched slay dozens of the kung fu genre's greatest, now patiently healing a multitude of people young and old on his massage tables was an unexpected but fitting image. His remedial work for a generation of youthful martial artists like myself through his films was not all that incompatible with the man he had become. Like the taxi driver in *Dynamo*, returning to his proletariat roots of service. "In Dynamo, I gave director Hua Shan the idea of how the character should go back and become a taxi driver again," he explained. "How he craves for a simple life at the end."

Somehow, that this was Ho's idea didn't surprise me at all.

When it was time to leave I shook his hand once again. I looked down noting for a moment this traditional form of greeting and farewell becoming a gesture of long overdue unity where one hand had helped shaped the other so many decades ago. Through martial training, through creativity, through youthful escapism and through the visualization that our dreams await us to be shaped into history when we just set ourselves on the path.

"In China, there's a saying, 'a man leaves a name behind him; but a tiger leaves a skin behind him'," he said with a smile that probably indicated he was wondering if I would get it. "I've always hoped that I can make contributions and that it would be honoured. So that people would know who I am."

I moved away back out into the night, the old street lights flickering along the crooked road ahead. I turned to look a final time at Ho behind me, adjusting an old rusted chair in front of his office before grabbing a broom to sweep away the debris at his feet. There is no more fitting of a finalé to one's

life than the reward of following a dream in a such a way that it rouses another, or maybe countless others, to enjoy their own. I know I don't walk alone on this path that began in my child, encouraged and impelled by Ho's performances and contributions to a cinema that has encouraged millions of artists of all kinds. We don't all get to meet our heroes, but I am grateful my own path led far enough to the doorstep of one just to take a moment and thank him.

(Elements of the article are part of the forthcoming Bruceploitation Bible *book* **by Worth)**

the ART of VENGEANCE

Drawings by Artist Ken Lee

My name is Ken Lee. I was born and raised in London.
Growing up Hong Kong cinema has always been part of my life, I still remember watching *School on Fire* on VHS and the sheer experience it gave me was unlike anything I had ever seen… Kung fu movies have also inspired me a lot, especially Bruce Lee and Donnie Yen, to name but a few, and also not forgetting the female leads such as Wai Ying-hung (Auntie), and Angelo Mao.

My parents are from Hong Kong but I was born and raised in the UK. I'm a self-taught artist and like most people started drawing as a kid.

I use b&w pencils, colour pencils, biro pen and colour ball point pens. Depending on the drawing it could be one media or more. I normally do a mix of solo portraits and compilations. I like to show fine details and precision, to use a wide variety of colours and display different facial expressions and postures.

Here I share some of my art related to this amazing genre. I hope you enjoy viewing them as much as I enjoyed drawing them.

POPS - BIRO PEN.

Cheng Pei Pei - colour pencils.

Bruce clones - biro pen.

Angela Mao

Auntie Wai Ying-Hung

Shaw Bros compilation - B&W pencils.

BRUCE LEE
Collector The U.S. Connection

by Andrew P. Bovell

Hello. My name is Andrew P. Bovell.

I grew up in Georgetown Guyana and had never seen nor heard of Bruce Lee or martial arts. My family came to the United States in 1971 at eleven years of age. Two weeks after arriving I was walking with my mother and saw a poster of Bruce Lee. I stared in fascination (his look and physique). One year later upon my family acquiring our first television I saw the trailer for *The Chinese Connection* and we were all blown away by what we saw.

My parents are very traditional so I wasn't allowed to go to the movies as they deemed me too young. My older brothers went to see *The Chinese Connection* and told me the entire plot of the movie word for word. I felt as if I had seen it. A month later my eldest brother brought home a Bruce Lee poster from *The Chinese Connection* and hung it in his room. I stared at that poster day after day until I needed to own it, so I bargained with him to do all his chores for one week for the poster. He agreed.

I didn't see my first Bruce Lee movie until I was fisteen years-old and my mother accompanied me to see what Bruce lee was about and why I was so taken with him. We saw *Return of the Dragon*. When we left the movie theatre she took me to the news stand and bought me every magazine he was on.

I have collected Bruce Lee memorabilia for the last forty-seven years. Quality is number one for me. Bruce Lee has gotten me through some extremely rough times and reminds me everyday to never give up, never doubt myself and never say NO to myself. Bruce Lee has been and always will be my hero. I love seeing his collectibles and fans who love, respect and appreciate Bruce Lee to the max.

I don't love, respect and admire Bruce Lee because I think he was the baddest dude on the planet. I hold him in the highest regards because he was the little engine who could and did. His spirit, his presence, his mind was so powerful he couldn't be ignored. He accomplished a lot in his short but effective life and in the end he reminds us that he, we are only human.

Long Live the spirit of Bruce Lee.

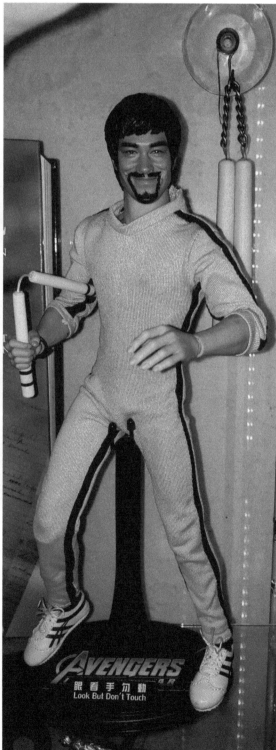

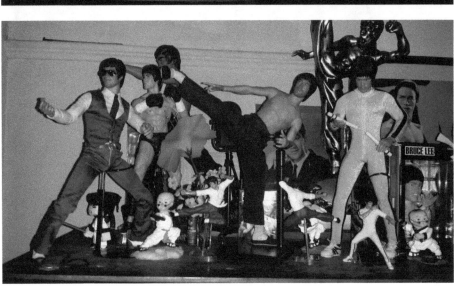

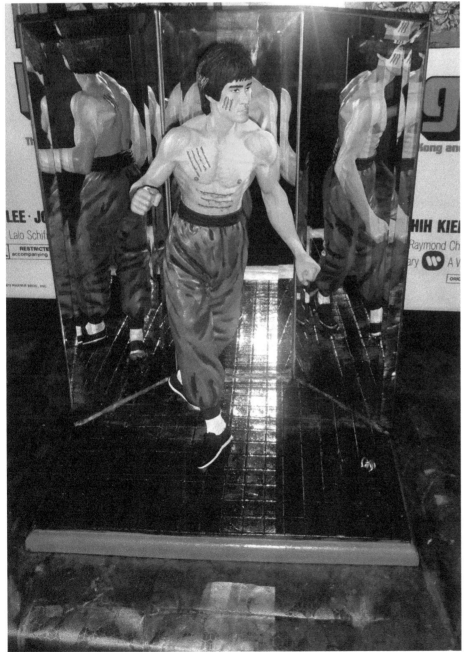

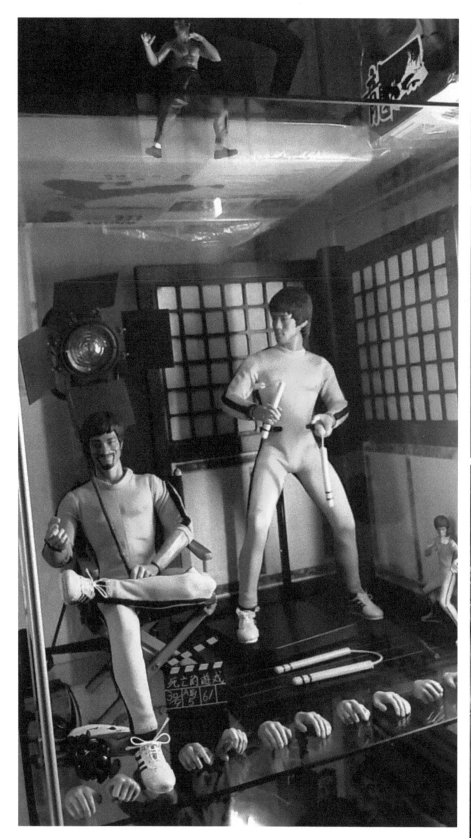

DREAM and SWORD

by Martin Sandison

Three Classics of Taiwanese Wuxia Pain Cinema

A couple of years ago I visited a fellow kung fu bro in Croatia, and I noticed a screensaver he had was of a movie called *Love and Sword*. I didn't know the title, and inquired about it. He waxed lyrical about the film, saying I had to see it. Shortly thereafter I purchased the Rarescope DVD second hand and settled down one night to watch it. The film that unfolded gladdened my eyes and heart; I was in awe of the brilliance of old school Asian cinema yet again, and had discovered another strand. The film is Taiwanese, and is my favourite example of their Wuxia Pain pictures. In this article I will extol the virtues of three of my favourites of the genre, ones that any fan of swordplay films must see.

Let's begin with **LOVE AND SWORD**, the cream of the crop I've seen outside of the master of the deepest martial arts films ever made, King Hu. His *A Touch Of Zen* and *Dragon Inn* stand tall as pinnacles of pure, spiritual cinema that transcend genre. An actor who appeared in both, Roc Tien-peng, is the star of *Love and Sword*. Hsiao Fang is a fabled swordsman who has fallen in love with Meng Yueh-hsin, a girl whose father was killed. Hsiao vows to kill all of those involved with his murder, encountering sword masters at every turn.

Being a Taiwanese Indie production, I expected a demonstrably low budget, and cheap-looking sets, like those I'd seen in films like the Pearl Chang Ling-starrer *My Blade, My Life*. As the first scenes began there was a sense of spectacle and aesthetic grace

that drew me in completely. If ever there was a genre to demonstrate how to use a low budget to your advantage, it's indie martial arts movies. *Love and Sword* creates a magnificently realised world, one that has room for flowing camerawork, beautifully constructed mise en scene and something that is a bit of a rarity; a concentration on character depth that is reflected in its visuals. Tien's motivations seem straightforward, but come to the end a twist creates real emotional depth, and is reflected so wonderfully visually that it brought a tear to my eye. Favouring widescreen compositions and atmospheric swirls of mist, the film is a real treat for the eyes. Interestingly it was director Yu Kan-ping's debut, a filmmaker who began his career as an assistant director on Wuxia Pain films such as The *Majestic Cat* and *Lost Samurai Sword*. He also worked in the Taiwan arm of Cinema City, and produced John Woo's early comedy *The Time You Need a Friend*.

tung (my favourite being the inimitable *Duel to the Death*) and John Woo's *Last Hurrah For Chivalry*; in fact, the end move that finishes off the villain is very similar to Woo's Wuxia Pain theme-setting opus. There are mind blowing combinations of kicking, beautiful intricacy in the sword exchanges, matched by pin-sharp editing. Action director Poon Yiu-kwan, who worked on *A Touch of Zen*, proves his worth completely. It's a shame he never moved higher, but then the history of martial arts movies is littered with great choreographers who never did; such as Hsu Hsia (*Five Superfighters*) and Taiwan's own Peng Kang (*Shaolin vs Lama*).

In *Love and Sword*, Roc Tien Peng completely outdoes himself in a performance of such charisma, vulnerability, and melancholy hidden behind his sword that it's one of my favourites in the pantheon of Wuxia Pain cinema. His introductory scene is a masterful dream-like sequence that is deep in its imagining. Most films of this type were made for pure entertainment, nothing wrong with that, but *Love and Sword* aims high, and is close to the sheer artistic brilliance of King Hu.

Love and Sword is a tragic love story as much as it is a story of combat, and is based on a novel by Gu Long, his works of course a source for so many Wuxia Pain films (such as *Death Duel*).

The movie has huge influence from King Hu in approach to visual style, emotional undercurrent and slowly swelling orchestration in the film's soundtrack. In turn *Love and Sword* can be seen to have inspired later classics such as Ronny Yu's new wave surrealistic swordplay epic *The Bride With the White Hair*.

As the narrative of *Love and Sword* progresses, the action steadily becomes more intricate and inventively filmed. It would be a fool to think this is on purpose; that an aim of the story was to reflect the interior of Roc Tien's suffering, and that as he slowly feels the weight of his conscience too much to bear, all he has is his sword and the moment, in which he is lost to instinct and always close to death. But, I would love to think this is the reason. Most probably, it was a production issue, and this

happens in countless martial arts films. I'd love to read a book dedicated to detailing the productions of these classics, but so little is known that it would be a mammoth task. The final two fights in *Love and Sword* are up there with the best of Ching Siu-

A TOUCH OF ZEN

ROY CHIAO, LEFT, AND HAN YING CHIEH IN KING HU'S *A TOUCH OF ZEN*

SWORD
OF JUSTICE

原著:古龍
編劇:倪匡
導演:李嘉

名劍煞流

Shang-liang and Tieh Yun getting drunk together yet retaining their stoic, dream-like expressions is redolent of the Taiwanese style, one that retains the tropes laid down by Shaw Brothers yet have their own surreal atmosphere. Like *Love and Sword* the aesthetic beauty of the film is one that creates a fully immersive world, with inventive framing and lighting of shots that is way ahead of most old school martial arts films. As most films in the genre go, the fights get better as they go along.

The final two-on-one is a sight to behold, with long shots and long takes mixed in with wirework, acrobatics, hardcore intricate exchanges and fantastic impactful editing. The invention also stretches to dramatic and death scenes, with one sticking out in my mind when a villain is slashed through his wooden bath, the blood flowing out of the hole in close up.

Director Hui Sing Ye had a short career, and before *Sword of Justice* made the Wuxia Pain film *Fight For Glory* starring the great Norman Tsui Siu-keung. That movie is high on my watchlist, and the talent and eye that Hui has on show in *Sword of Justice* means I'll give his whole filmography a try. Ching Pang, aswell as putting in a great crazed performance as the villain, doubles

as the film's fight choreographer, and sadly didn't do a lot of work otherwise. It's criminal, with the chops he shows in front of and behind the camera. Liu Shang-chien gives a performance for the ages as Lung Sang-liang, imbuing him with just the right amount of mystique, charisma, depth and excellent sword skills. Liu appeared in a lot of movies from the '70s onwards, even starring as the Monkey King in a 1982 adaptation of the classic Chinese myth.

While *Sword of Justice* doesn't quite achieve the balance between character depth, story and visuals that *Love and Sword* does, Lung Sang-liang's journey is one that will keep you watching. Liu Shang-chien's performance hits all the right notes, and alongside the other actors helps communicate the surreal twists on classical Wuxia Pain that the Taiwanese were so adept at achieving.

Made in 1980, one year after *Love and Sword*, **SWORD OF JUSTICE** came to my attention through Alan Donkin's article on movie posters in the last issue of *Eastern Heroes*. His description of the film made me immediately want to track it down. Thanks again to my friend from Croatia, I received a download. The first thing that struck me was just how faded and worn the print I saw was. I would doubt this film has ever had a release in the West, and a collector adapted their film print to digital. You know what? The condition of the print drew me even more into the dream-like odyssey of a story the picture tells, the hallucinatory web of the old style weaving its indelible charm.

The narrative of the film is more like a series of vignettes until the middle section begins; the protagonist Lung Shang-liang encounters swordsmen and women who he must defeat to gain the titular sword of justice. Come the middle he befriends a fellow swordsman Tieh Yun and both must combine to kill the evil and insane Shuah Yu-liu.

Sword of Justice is full of the martial chivalry and loyalty that the best of the genre contains, as it would be with Gu Long credited as a planner. Scenes of Lung

DRAGON INN.

As many of us know Shaw Brothers adaptations of Gu Long's novels were at times hugely complex affairs with many characters introduced, with a lot of them not serving any purpose in the loose narratives. Taiwan's **A SWORD NAMED REVENGE** utilises this type of approach, but actually manages to incorporate many characters that serve to develop the plot, and weaves its story strands with purpose and logic, unlike a lot of the Shaw Brothers interpretations of the maestro novelist's works.

Yu Pei-yu is the son of a renowned master, and in the opening scene is the only survivor of a bloody massacre at his house. Shortly afterwards some other members of the sect come back and encounter Yu's father whom You had seen killed with his own eyes. He recounts the story to his friends, but his father's body has disappeared. Yu escapes and wanders the land in sadness and near-insanity. He comes across Red Lily, a wandering vagabond who wants to help. Soon Yu is back in his right mind, and must work out who is the interloper who has taken on his father's identity, encountering those who help and hinder him in his travels.

As well as having an above-average script and story, *A Sword Named Revenge* fits firmly into the Taiwanese Wuxia Pain mould. Dream-like scenes, set ups and acting, powerfully atmospheric lighting and intricate sword fights are the order of the day. One of my favourite scenes involves

a little person who burns down his house when he discovers Yu with his wife, laughing maniacally as he does so. This bizarre style of designing characters is a trademark of Gu Long, and here it is explored brilliantly. The film also manages to maintain a consistently melancholic yet hard edged tone, despite some silly scenes involving a fat master in the middle section.

The movie is directed by Lee Chia, who also made *The Lost Swordship*, a pretty good film in the same genre, and a bunch of other stuff previously. On choreographer duties is Suen Shu-pau, who by this time had the shapes classic *7 Commandments of Kung Fu*, and other good credits such as *Buddha's Palm and Dragon's Fist*, under his belt. His work here, especially in the end fight, is as good as anything in the Wuxia Pain genre. Wirework and backwards photography is more prevalent than in the previous two films in this article, and it's all the better for it. Like *Love and Sword*, the investment in story and character means the combat is made more powerful and adrenalin-pumping, with you really rooting for Yu Pei-yu and Red Lily.

As Yu, Champ Wang is a name and face many of you will recognise. He was usually a bit-part actor in many old schoolers, my favourites being *Green Jade Statuette* and *Devil Killer*. Here he absolutely shines, showing his acting and martial abilities. Kao Chiang as Red Lily, an archetypal character of which a variation appears in most Gu Long works, has real depth to his performance and the final farewell between the two is beautifully filmed. Two female characters played by Li Hsuan and Shally Yue San respectively add colour and romance to the plotline.

The rich expressive beauty of Taiwanese Wuxia Pain is reflected in my three picks; but there are also many more quality productions of the time to explore. These include *Dream Sword*, starring starring

Lung Fei wielding an axe, and Yueh Hua. Director Chang Peng Yi's sequence of movies with titles such as *Blade of Doom* and *The Clutch of Power* are all worth a watch. There are also many more I've still to see, and it excites me no end that they are out there just waiting for me to take in. This is a controversial statement, but for me the Taiwanese productions extend beyond what most Shaw Brothers productions were doing in Hong Kong at the same time. Hey, life would be boring if we all had the same opinions. If you've not seen these films and have a love for Wuxia Pain, I would be delighted if you gave them a try, and see if they spark the love like they have done for me.

CLUTCH OF POWER

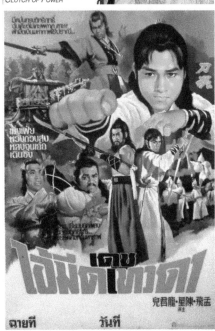

COMING JANUARY 2022

Enter THE CROW

by Hector Martinez

Brandon 'Bruce' Lee was just twenty-eight years old when he fell victim to one of the most tragic and incomprehensible accidents that eventually took his life on March 31st, 1993 in Wilmington, North Carolina during the filming of James O'Barr's screen adaptation of his gothic underground comic book *The Crow*.

From the very beginning of the production, accidents were happening almost on a day to day basis with unexplained occurrences plaguing the set. Oh yes, twenty-seven years later after its release and *The Crow* continues to have its share of controversy and mystery! What I find intriguing is that although several times a remake has been attempted (even the lead for the part has been chosen) yet almost immediately the attempts vaporize into thin air. I believe that the reason a remake has never materialized is because *The Crow* is to Brandon Lee what *Enter The Dragon* was to his father, they were both predestined to star in these films and no one nor nothing will ever fill those shoes.

The first time I saw Brandon was on television back in February 1st, 1986 during his acting debut in *Kung Fu: The Movie* which was made for television. In it Brandon plays the part of 'Chung Wang' (Kwai Chang Caine's son) and aired on his birthday. I especially love the scene when Brandon appears in the rain standing in the front of the house looking for Caine, I couldn't believe how much he looked like his father in his 1957 film *The Thunderstorm* with such striking movie star good looks.

In 1987 a pilot was created by CBS as a follow up to the *Kung Fu* television series called *Kung Fu: The Next Generation* but sadly was never made into a series. By this time I forgot about Brandon and continued

watching my Bruce Lee films on vhs. I do remember stopping by a video store in our New York's Chinatown and saw a vhs copy to Brandon's first and only Hong Kong film *Legacy of Rage* which was produced in 1986 but in spite of the impression he left in

me from his performance in *Kung Fu: The Movie* I didn't bother to pick it up so I left it on the shelf.

But in 1991 my interest in Brandon took a turn for the very best and to what would lead to ultimately finding a place in my

ALL PHOTOS COURTESY OF AL LEONG

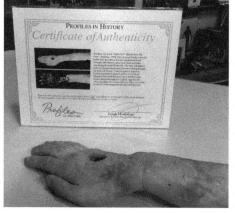

tragic is that we lost Brandon much too young and during a time when his 'star' was about to shine brighter.

You will read about this here first: A friend of mine told me a story of his chance meeting with Brandon Lee at the collectable toy shop he worked at here in New York City back in 1992, he says the day was slow and quiet and a tall young man with hair almost down to his shoulders walks in and quietly starts admiring the vintage toys in the display cases. After a few minutes my friend asks the guest if he needed help with anything and the guest turns around and politely says "Just looking around, thank you." Well, to his amazement my friend recognizes that the guest is Brandon Lee. So he steps out from behind the counter and walks up to Brandon, introduces himself and goes on to say how much he's admired his father and goes on to congratulation him on the success of his two major films.

After some talk about the store and its collectibles my friend asks Brandon if he's working on a new project to which Brandon responds "Yes, my next film is *The Crow*, I'll be playing a musician by the name of Eric Draven."

My friend immediately recognized the comic book and its author James O'Barr and he congratulated Brandon on such a terrific project and wished him success to which Brandon responds "It's going to be an exciting film but I won't live to see it."

My friend held on to that experience with Brandon for a number of years but when the toy shop came to its end he decided it was time to share it with me.

super confident and with similar gestures just like his famous dad! Then a year later came *Rapid Fire* (1992) and Brandon was officially a star!

Since the passing of his father Bruce Lee, gone were the days of when going to the movies was extra special, when my friends and I saw the trailers to the new Bruce Lee films that were coming to our local movie theatres and didn't stop talking about it until the day came to finally see it! And now, that thrill and excitement was back all due to Brandon Lee!

What's sad, disappointing and downright

collection for Brandon. As I sat in the movie theater electricity and anticipation filled the air very much the same as when I sat to watch *Fists of Fury* (*The Big Boss*) back in 1973 but this time it was for Brandon Lee's debut in his first major American film *Showdown in Little Tokyo* and instantly Brandon became the rightful 'heir' to his father's throne! He was charismatic,

After Brandon's passing I started to search out various projects he had done, interviews, TV show appearances and came across a 1990 film which had Brandon teaming up with veteran actor Ernest Borgnine for a low budget film shot in Germany called *Laser Mission* which got a small run in theatres but to my knowledge was never screened in New York City so this one went hiding under the radar. I did get to see it on video after the success of his three major films and *Laser Mission* (with its share of shortcomings) is now a personal favourite!

In recent years Brandon Lee and *The Crow* have gained an even larger following through the various collectables which have recently been released from companies like Hot Toys, Diamond Select and Sideshow.

Although most hardcore Bruce Lee collectors I know do not collect Brandon Lee, to me Brandon will forever be a very important part of the Bruce Lee legacy, and because of my respect and interest in Brandon's career I will continue to help keep his memory alive through my collection of ephemera.

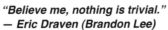

"Believe me, nothing is trivial."
— Eric Draven (Brandon Lee)

FROM CUB TIGER TO VANGUARD

By Paul Dre
(The Jackie Chan Appreciation Facebook Group)

PART 2

JACKIE CHAN - Longevity of a Legend

WELCOME BACK EVERYONE! The time has come to buckle back up in the nearest Mitsubishi vehicle you can find and don that JC stunt team attire you have lurking in the bottom draw, gloves un'all... as this is going to be bumpy ride, as we follow Jackie through his early troublesome years of his life as a stuntman in Part 2 of 'Cub Tiger to Vanguard'.

(WARNING) reading fanzine articles is no light work, expect to experience the possibility of minor eye strain, migraine like symptoms, although unlike Jackie (should you avoid any descents from your kitchen stool) – free from fractures.

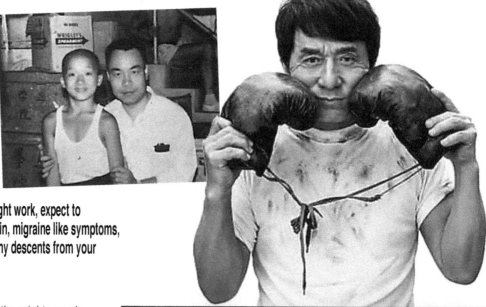

Now, before we furiously start chanting the mighty words.... yī (1), èr (2) … sān (3) followed by a nose dive into those dusty apple boxes, that even your local supermarket would have second thoughts as to, if they were worthy enough for the waste baler.

Firstly, I consider it appropriate that we allow opportunity to acknowledge the very sad and most recent passing of two screen greats, Roy Horan on the 12th October 2021 (Aged 71) and Dean Shek 劉偉成 (aka Shek Tien / Dean Shek Tin) on the 31st October 2021. Both have been pivotal figures in the Hong Kong film industry and their contributions will forever be our pleasure.

Roy Horan, a name that is renowned to fans of Hong Kong martial arts cinema. Roy is arguably best known for his appearance as 'Lewis' from 1981's *Tower of Death* 死亡塔 (aka *Game of Death 2*) and the Russian Priest "Jesus… he's a sinner!!!" starring alongside Jackie Chan and Hwang Jang-lee in seasonal's 1978 smash hit *Snake in the Eagle's Shadow* 蛇形刁手.

Dean Shek to Chan fans is most well known for his classic appearances in *Fearless Hyena* 1 and 2, *Snake in the Eagle's Shadow*, *Drunken Master*, *Half a Loaf of Kung Fu* and *Master With Cracked fingers*.

As well as a fine actor, Dean was also a writer, producer, director and one of the founders of the renowned Cinema City company, that kept Golden Harvest on their toes during the glory years.

Nowadays, as alluded to in Part 1, Jackie Chan 成龍 is one of the most famous men in the world. Wherever Chan goes he's mobbed by fans of all cultures, backgrounds and ages, fans like me, who are just desperate to get a glimpse of the man that has been such a positive and consistent influence in our lives. In fact for many the name Jackie Chan resembles more than that of an individual of heroic stature, rather a feeling of family and sense of community.

Although today and for a considerable time, Jackie has been a household name globally. The early years however, were not always so bright as the budding martial arts Pao Pao was soon to discover.

You would think that an individual that possessed the skills Jackie had acquired early in life at the Peking Opera School would likely be well and truly set on a road to stardom, which couldn't be further from the truth for Jackie.

Jackie's father Charles Chan was a cook and his mother a housekeeper for the commissioner of the French embassy in Hong Kong. Back then young Jackie (Kong Sang) lived with his parents in a small room in the back of the commissioners mansion. Jackie's first introduction to martial arts was from his father who taught him Northern style Siu Hung Kun Kung Fu every morning. It's only natural for a father to want to teach his son, but Chan soon become mischievous and started getting into fights. Jackie in essence went from 'Brat to Brawler' in a short period of time. This lead to a short attempt of enrolment at the elementary academy followed by his arrival at the China Drama Academy Opera School. Jackie favoured kung fu to academics, 'A sore body was better than a numb brain'. A phrase that was to transpire into a way of life for Jackie.

Life in front of the camera kick started in the 1960s for Jackie, when he was frequently lent out to film studios whenever they needed some children in the background. Of course any money earned went straight to Master Yuen's pocket to pay for their tuition.

Keeping a tally for all of Jackie's screen appearances is no simple feat, according to some sources,

it has been suggested that Jackie may have been in as many of twenty-five films by the time he was ten years old, though even Jackie doesn't know what most of them were! More commonly known and frequently referenced are that of *Big and little Wong Tin Bar* 大小黃天霸 whereby an eight year old Jackie was cast alongside the great Taiwanese star Li Li-hua. To follow was the likes of the Shaw Brothers film *The Love Eterne* 梁山伯與祝英台 and *The Story of Qiu Xiang Lin*. For many years historians have cited a child Chan appearance in *Come Drink with Me*, to which is incorrect and has likely been asserted in confusion.

In the early 1970s, opera schools were closing down as there wasn't enough interest to keep them going, Jackie and his classmates all went to find film work, taking with them the years of experiences and extraordinary athleticism. Many of his classmates all went on to have distinguished film careers themselves including Sammo Hung, Yuen Biao, Yuen Wah and Corey Yuen.

The boys from Peking started out as stuntmen for hire. They'd hang around the film studios everyday hoping they be one of the lucky ones to find paid work that day.

At the time, Jackie's father Charles was hoping he would live with his parents in Australia, however the young cub tiger had ulterior ideas and was determined to make it on his own.

It was Big Brother 大哥 Sammo Hung (formerly known as Yuen Lung) who helped a young Jackie through various introductions, as the young Sammo was doing pretty well for himself being able to work with friends whenever he needed to, so he introduced Jackie, after all they were considered brothers, and so it was he worked on King Hu's *A Touch of Zen* 俠女.

Jackie found himself in a close circuit of networking allowing work as an extra and stuntmen opportunities. Unfortunately, nobody, even Jackie himself seems to know the names of all his early stunt work films, sadly we may never know the true inventory of such work.

To succeed as a stuntman was not merely limited to having the guts required to place your body or even direct your body into the path of harms way. The industry was a tough and the standards were high. Jackie worked tirelessly on the film sets, determined to make a difference among a sea of many. Stunts shot that were not deemed satisfactory for film meant that was a risk to the stuntman that they would not be paid for their efforts and also render their use for work on the following shoot. Fortunately for Jackie, this was an area of work in which he excelled and thus then working ethos of 'never give up' was born.

Whilst working at the renowned Shaw Brothers studio, Jackie was to embark on his first most significant mature appearances on film. Jackie appeared two movies at this time by director Ho Meng-hua which was to be entitled *Lady of Steel* and *Ambush*. Jackie soon became a recognisable face at the Golden Harvest studios during the early 1970s, continuing to blend between Shaw Brothers and Golden Harvest for stuntman appearances, the young Chan had developed an ability to be killed well, action directors liked his ability to act and fall down dead. Now having mastered being a dead body, Jackie's body of work (no pun intended) started to flourish further with stunt appearances in the likes of *Village of Tigers*, *Angry River* and *The Blade Spares None*.

Bumps, abrasions and bruises aplenty, the young Pao Pao continued to push his body through the demands of rigorous stuntwork. Jackie was known to often volunteer for the most dangerous stunt and he was soon beginning to start turning the

right heads in his direction. The legendary Bruce Lee was soon to recognise Chan's undeniable talents, when Jackie performed the most dangerous stunt in Bruce Lee's *Fist of Fury* 精武門 directed by Lo Wei, whom was soon to become an important figure in Jackie's advancing career. Jackie also appeared as a stuntman in the Bruce Lee masterpiece *Enter the Dragon* – getting to know the end of Lee's escrima sticks, on a personal level as it sank into his head and having his neck snapped by Lee during battle.

"ALMOST EVERY MOVIE SET, FIGHTING... FIGHTING...FIGHTING!! NO REASON BUT THE WAY YOU LOOK AT ME, THEN KEEP FIGHTING, FIGHT TEN MINUTES - AUDIENCE GETTING BORING!!" – Jackie Chan 1989
The Incredibly Strange Film Show

Jackie, alongside many of his Opera buddies, enjoyed screen time and stuntwork in the Jimmy Shaw produced *Fist of Unicorn* 麒麟掌 starring Unicorn Chan. Jimmy being the sharp man he was sure to incorporate Bruce Lee to help promote and sell this movie, fans reading this article will no doubt be familiar with this project

regarding Bruce. The director print credits state the movie is directed by Tong Dik, Tong being the opera master to the great 'Mars' (looking absolutely fighting fit here – Mars in lean mode), although it is believed this was a co-directed picture with Shin Hwa-cook 曲興華.

Cook was a good friend of Jackie's and cited as being his godfather. It is considered that perhaps Cook was responsible for pulling in Jackie for his stunt performances in the *Fist of Unicorn*.

Whilst the above only serves to skim the surface of Jackie's contributions to stuntwork within the Hong Kong film industry during this era, it cannot be denied

that the projects he worked on between 1971 and 1973 were starting to shape in significance.

During such years Jackie was fortunate to be able to step up his game by increasing his on-screen time appearances and landed more prominent roles with the Great Earth Movie Company in titles such as *Police Woman* 女警察 (aka *Here Comes Big Brother* / *The Herione* / *Young Tiger* / *Rumble in Hong Kong*) where Chan played a villain and *Not scared to Die* (aka *Fist of Anger* / *Eagle Shadow Fist*). Jackie appeared in his first starring role as the main hero lead in *Cub Tiger from Kwang Tung*.

Cub Tiger from Kwang Tung 广东 小老虎 known to many as the cheap, unsuccessfully dire movie that only served as any use when it was later signed to Dick Randall in 1979 for its splice and dice makeover treatment to the later reincarnated cult effort known as *Master with Cracked Fingers* (aka *Master with Crack Fingers* / *Snake Fist Fighter*).

If you were to form your opinion soley on how *Cub Tiger* has been depicted in sources over the years, you'd probably never bother to watch it, unless of course, like me – you're a die hard Chan fan – and whilst I should be clear this movie is by no means an award winning work of art and is liable to be flawed at many corners, from its lesser production values and the well documented working conditions.

However, it should be remembered that this was a very important project for Jackie, to reflect back to that time and noting Jackie's age – this was a big deal for the young cub. Jackie had an enormous weight of responsibility on his shoulders for such tender years, as he performed the role of lead star and served as action director – this movie could actually be considered as ahead of its time in many ways.

Jackie is evidently trying hard in the movie and you can feel his effort through the screen. Jackie was trying to find his own ground in a world that was dominated by the Martial Arts King Bruce Lee. The youthful teenage Chan can be seen bouncing around the screen, whilst letting loose a frenzy of some of the best combination kicks and flips ever seen in

his movies. It is also clear that even back then he was finding innovative ways to use the environment in his fight scenes and the fight on the Dock as he goes toe-to-toe against Chan Hung-lit 陳鴻烈 has some great moments.

The scene that stands out the most to me from *Cub Tiger from Kwang Tung* as pure Jackie Chan is the scene with co-star Tien Feng where Jackie is catching ceramic flower pots – by any means possible – that are being projected at him from Tien. I find it incredible that in that very moment, the Jackie Chan we have all come to love over the years, was truly evident. In fact it's a physical gag that Jackie has reused countless times throughout his career in variations over time such as within the movies *Fearless Hyena* 笑拳怪招, *Battle Creek Brawl*, *Rush Hour* and *Shanghai Knights* just to name a few.

So whilst *Cub Tiger* in unlikely to start blowing minds some fifty odd years after its release, it surely holds up as a fine testament to the birth of a legend and the working morales to which he would forever strive for.

Stunt work has been the bread and butter of Jackie's trade which only blossomed to greater heights in 1980s as Jackie commenced an upgrade to his daredevil antics. When looking back at his very early efforts, to which I shall single out *Police Woman* or should I say, the '90s *Rumble in the Bronx* cash-in title / re-release *Rumble in Hong Kong* (to which is secretly my favoured title). Jackie pulls out the big guns with some incredibly impressive stunts in this straight-up 1970s gangland crime flick. Such unsung stunts include scaling outbuildings to evade a pursuing car and jumping onto a moving car roof, minus any umbrellas!

When you couple these stunts and physical gags that I have referred to from *Cub Tiger* and *Police Woman* by the time we have even reached 1973, the trademarks of the living legend are there to be seen and formed the foundations of what was to follow.

As we progress into the mid 1970s Jackie continued to appear in small supporting roles in titles such as *Golden Lotus* 金瓶雙艷, *The Himalayan*, *All in the Family* and *No End of Surprises* as a savage female serial killer. Next for Jackie was to be another step into a positive direction when he landed a spear-fighting supporting role in the John Woo directed kung fu classic *Hand of Death* 少林門 (1975) (aka *Countdown in Kung Fu*). Kung fu mayhem aplenty, Chan had the opportunity to dominate his screen time by dazzling the

audience with his spear-fu performances, showing that he was even more capable when it came to wielding weapons, *Hand of Death* also allowed Jackie the chance to perform some work and learn new skills with the use of horses, which again would

see a return later in his career. Jackie has never been one to turn down any opportunity to learn a new skill to bring to the movies and being the quick learner he was and physicality he possessed, this was never a problem for Chan. Post *Hand of Death* Jackie then went onto to assist with fight choreography on the Angela Mao Ying movie *Dance of Death* (1976)舞拳.

As alluded to in Part 1 of my article, Jackie took a slight pause in his career after *Hand of Death* to return to Australia to be with his parents, fearing that stardom was never going to be his destiny as he failed to make the impact he longed for. When I say a pause, I mean only a slight pause, few months went by, he was then to receive a telegram from an instrumental figure that was to change his life, for the better.

Although Jackie was already considering his return, he received a telegram from Mr Willie Chan 陳自強 in Hong Kong. Willie had just recently left Cathay Films to work as general manager for Lo Wei's newly formed production company. Jackie had written to Willie along with other people who were in the business to say he was going to Australia and Willie had remembered him. They were looking for someone to star in a sequel to the Bruce Lee classic *Fist of Fury* to which Jackie has already appeared in as a stuntman, and although Jackie didn't want to be the NEW Bruce Lee, it was a job and a step in the right direction.

Jackie flew back to his Hong Kong hood and signed a multi picture contract with Lo Wei. First up being *New Fist of Fury* 新精武門 (1976) directed by original FOF director, Lo Wei.

New Fist of Fury 新精武門 unfortunately was a flop, not an awful movie, but at that time it had all been done before and better. Bruce Lee had recently passed and Jackie at that time wasn't filling the void, neither did he want to. You see, Jackie… or Jacky as I should be correctly referring to at this point, was a great fan of the old black and white classics of Charlie Chaplin,

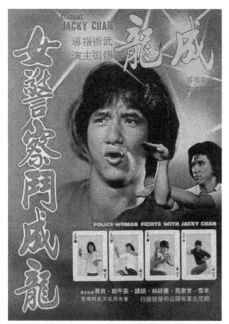

Buster Keaton and Harold Lloyd and really admired their work and wanted to make the audience feel the same way when they watched his movies as he felt watching theirs.

Jackie never wanted to be the superhero, Jackie wanted to be the underdog and for people to feel the pain he was enduring and sympathise with him and cheer for him when he's winning. But for now, he was stuck with what Lo Wei wanted, which was a new Bruce Lee.

"NOBODY CAN BE AS GOOD AS BRUCE, EVEN IN REALITY YOU CAN BE BETTER, YOU FIGHT BETTER, YOU KICK BETTER , YOU CAN NEVER BE BRUCE... SO LET'S MAKE KUNG FU COMEDY, YOU KNOW LETS, LET'S GIVE IT ANOTHER TREATMENT ...AND I GUESS HE JUST, WHAT YOU SAY? HIT THE NAIL ON THE HEAD."
– Willie Chan 1989
The Incredibly Strange Film Show

New Fist of Fury has likely been reborn to some extent to a newer audience more recently with thanks to the UK Blu-Ray release by 88 Films. The Blu-Ray offers a truly impressive transfer of the movie, marking its greatest appearance on a media format to date. This has allowed new fans who maybe viewing this movie for the first time in 2021 with the cleanest of lenses and for the older fans that have known the movie since the former video VHS roots have endured a heightened experience, for the most part. Anyway, I digress, I shall avoid talking about media formats just yet as I will be looking to explore the collectable media impact in due course as the journey progresses.

New Fist of Fury is like marmite to many, hate it… love it… with some that are indifferent. How about for me? Silly question? Of course, I love *New Fist of Fury* and consider it a little Jackie gem! Reiterating the comments for *Cub Tiger* several years prior, *NFOF* is Jackie's second opportunity to take centre stage so to speak, as a lead star at the age of twenty-two and I if the pressure was not already high… this was to be the star in a direct sequel to the legendary Bruce Lee! The shoes to fill were large.

Jacky being Jacky, gave it his all and certainly demonstrated his ability and despite the above pressures still managed to squeeze in some of that 'Chan Charm' that he would later own. Following its flop, Lo Wei handed the reigns to new director Chen Chi-hwa for the next film *Shaolin Wooden Men* 少林木人巷 (aka *Shaolin Chamber of Death* / *Wooden Men*).

Shaolin Wooden Men 少林木人巷 was said to be Jackie's dream project at that time having had much more freedom on the shoot and he and Chen got on very well and shared many similar ideas, the finished film was far better than *NFOF*, yet it still flopped at the box office.

It's a real shame as the movie is a thoroughly enjoyable kung fu adventure and holds up well to this very day as genre classic. There are many sequences in this film that are very impressive, in no small part due to Jackie co-choreographing the martial arts. Shapes fans are quick to cite

this movie as one of Jackie's late night kung fu classics – best served in a theatre full of whistle-wielding fans!

In an effort to recoup back some lossed money at the box office, Lo Wei took Jackie to Korea where film making was cheap to produce and what followed was the attempt of casting Jackie as a villain against the One-Armed Swordsman Jimmy Wang Yu 王羽 in the kung fu period basher *Killer Meteors* 風雨雙流星.

Meteors was shot in 1976, but not actually released until '78 at which time it was another box office flop. Whilst Chan portrayed the role of the poisoned Imortal Metoer, in reality Chan himself was trying to cling on to dear life from the media backlash of being considered box office poisen at this time.

Mocked by his peers and deflated by box office figures, it seemed no matter what Jackie done he was just not appealing to the audiences of the era. Bruce Lee was still very much the man and Jackie knew if he was too succeed an alternative route was needed, that route was to be himself, the first Jackie Chan.

STILL TO COME…
Follow the journey of the 'Cub Tiger to Vanguard' as we continue to explore the Lo Wei era and unbeknown to Jacky, he is to be moments away from box office records that were set to leave the likes of Bruce Lee blockbusters *Fist of Fury*, *Way of the Dragon* and *Enter the Dragon* in the dust !

Also to follow, Jackie's path to success continues as we advance through to the 1980s era, whereby Jackie's impact in the United Kingdom and worldwide was starting to send shock waves as he single handle started to define a whole new genre of movie making.

In the meantime I wish you all the best, stay safe…over and out. *Let's keep the JC flame shining bright.*

This article is dedicated in the memory of, Roy Horan (January 1st 1950 – October 12th 2021)
Dean Shek (October 17th 1950 – October 31st)

CINEMA OF HATE
For a Few BASHERS More

Another update review, on Old School Bashers, from the early '70s.

The Magnificent Boxer 我要持到底 (1973)

Aka: Shadow of the Dragon

Origin: Hong Kong

Cast: Charles Heung, Yukio Someno, Sun Lan-hon, Kwok Choi

by Andy Smith

Chen Shao-hwa (Cheng Lei), before leaving his kung fu school to go off to get married, recollects and shares his story on how he had won a boxing championship. Defeating representatives from different countries, he also adds Bolo to his list of beaten opponents (who makes a brief appearance in the movie). On the ship to his destination, he interrupts some cheating at a gambling table run by Master Tanake (Someno). This was proved not to be a good move.

Someno shows interest in buying a house, to set up a gambling den, but the owner (Shao Hwa's mother) won't sell, and so he sends his gang to pay her and the daughter a visit.

At another gambling joint, Someno and his gang are again rigging the table, and taking all the winnings. Skinny Guy – (Sun Lan) gets picked up off the streets, to help out the Someno crew with getting the house that he is trying to buy.

Shao Hwa doesn't get in contact with his teacher and his fellow students. Charles Heung is sent to check on him, as he seems to have gone missing. Charles notices a ring that was given to Shao Hwa, on the finger of one of Someno's men, and goes after him. Charles Heung and Someno brawl it out in a twelve minute end fight, where Someno meets his inevitable, and violent demise.

Charles Hueng is the hard hitting 'Magnificent Boxer. Yukio Someno plays the role of the gang boss. There are a few light comedy scenes with Sun Lan and Hon Kwok-choi, both displaying some clumsy fighting skills, as they both regularly clash. This is an entertaining kung fu basher, which deserves credit for the array of fight exchanges, and film cast is able to get away after beating them up inside an ambulance. He escapes and recovers in a nearby villa, where Elaine comes to visit. One of Junior's gang buddies is captured and tortured by White Tiger's men, forcing him to disclose the whereabouts of Blackbeard's hideout.

Both gangs subsequently end up in a shootout, and punch up. Blackbeard calls Junior for his assistance, and he goes off to help rescue his boss. White Tiger and his gang pursue in a car chase, but Junior escapes. Sadly, Elaine is discovered at Junior's place, and captured. Junior sets out to find her, but is also captured and beaten by the White Tiger crew. The case with money again changes hands, but Junior is this time tied up, battered and forced to watch Elaine being raped. Junior and Elaine are rescued by a friend, Tan Dun. Junior, in rage, vows to seek revenge.

Junior and Tan hunts down the White Tiger gang. The gang links some heavies and makes plans to travel by ship, to Japan. Tan single handedly attacks them as they prepare to leave. Junior and Elaine turn up, and a mass brawl begins, which finally ends on a bridge. Tan Dun is thrown off the side. White Tiger is defeated, and the movie ends with Junior being fatally wounded and meeting his tragic demise.

This is a high adrenaline and entertaining movie, with James Nam playing an excellent leading role. The script is fast paced, and was sometimes hard to follow, but nevertheless a very good bone crunching basher. The English audio dubbing makes the viewing easy, with a fine array of sound track snippets from *Shaft*, and others. Also, there are some interesting weapons on display, including a BBQ fork and gardening tools. A classic that needs to be viewed, at least once.

Deadly Fists 蓋世拳 (1972)
Aka: Revenge of the Iron Fist Maiden Taiwan

Origin: Taiwan

Cast: Chiang Pin, Wong Gam-fung, Sun Chia-Lin, Yi Yuan, Tien Yeh

A great intro to this movie, with silhouette characters fighting up close, to the *Shaft* soundtrack.

The pretty Sun Chia-lin (Feng Feng) discovers her father in a field, where he has been badly beaten and left to die. Feng Feng goes to the temple and tells the abbot that her father has been killed, and that she wants to seek revenge. She leaves to try and find out the motives. Her investigation takes her to Yi Yuan, whose men later pursue her. She is spared, when a fight is interrupted by Lung (Kung Bun), who fends off the gang and defeats one of the Japanese samurais. The samurai boss (Tien Yei) and his buddy Yi Yuan, vows to sort out Lung. Yuan uses his daughter, the likeable Hsiao Pei, to get friendly with Lung, and use him to find a missing treasure map. Yi Yuan tries to find Lung, whilst he is away. Lung returns to find that his uncle has been killed. Hsiao Pei uses her deceitful Delilah tactics to get hold of Lung's treasure map, after she lies about the uncle's killer. Lung is surrounded, beaten and captured. With only half the map found, and when he fails to disclose the whereabouts of the second half of the map, Yi Yuan's men burn his hands in hot oil.

Feng Feng breaks into the torture room and rescues Long. Yuan beats his daughter Hsiao Pei for not telling where Lung is hiding out. He sends his men to search the temple where Lung is

recovering. Yuan goes loopy when he finds out that his daughter is pregnant and Lung being the father. Lung trains, and recovers from his injuries. Yuan and Tien find out where Lung is hiding, before hunting him down.

In the end, both Lung and Feng Feng engage the in a deadly epic fight with Tien Wei and Yuan.

This is a high level basher, based on its script and martial arts action. In my opinion, it gets a five star rating, as it has to be up there as one of the best bashers ever! The cast, nice execution of the fighting sequences, makes this essential viewing.

Tough Guy 硬漢 (1972)

UK Title: Kung Fu the Head Crusher
US Title: Revenge of the Dragon

Origin: Hong Kong

Cast: Chen Sing, Cheung Lik,
Henry Yu Yong, San Yun

Martial Arts Director: Yuen Woo-ping

The story goes something like this… A couple of cops (Chen Sing and Cheung Lik) are tasked with an undercover operation, to go to over East Cloud Fort, infiltrate a drug gang, and take down the leader Lao San-hu (Sun Lan). Chen Sing gets himself locked up in the same prison as one of Lau San Hu's henchmen – Tang Lung. Both Chen Sing and Tang Lung forge a friendship on the inside, and then make their escape together. Cheung Lik goes to the town, and pretends to be a simple villager. They both plan to meetup later.

On unloading a dodgy shipment of cargo, a worker gets picked on by one of the gang. Henry Yu Yong intervenes to help, and a fight breaks out on the waterfront. Chen Sing steps in to help and beats up the foreman, along with the rest of his lackies. Chen Sing becomes friends with Henry Yu Yong, and is invited back to Yong's yard.

Lao San-hu hires Tang Lung to kill Chen Sing, but in an encounter, Tang Lung realizes that Chen Sing was his old prison buddy, and persuades him to join their gang. Chen soon gets involved in the gang's wrong doings, but despises the extortion tactics. On hearing that Chen has teamed up with Tang Lung, Henry Yu Yong feels betrayed, and is pissed with the news that he is now working for the gang's boss.

Chen is suspected as being a cop, spying on operations. Another shipment arrives at the pier, where they end up in another fight. Cheung Lik boards a junk to investigate the cargo, and gets found out. Another mass brawl ends up on the waterfront, where Chen has to stage Cheung Lik's death, so as not to blow his own cover. Lau San Hu plots to capture Chen. He is finally outnumbered in a warehouse, where he is beaten and tortured. Yu Yong and Cheung Lik are both ambushed, with Yu Yong's sister getting killed at the same time.

Chen escapes in chains and begins to crush a few skulls. Lao San-hu and his gang run off. Chen fights with Tang Lung to the end, where the horrid Lao San-hu is apprehended and supposedly arrested.

This classic from 1972 is a serious basher, despite some lighthearted comedy

TOUGH GUY

scenes, where Lao San Hu struggles to perform in the bedroom. The action is exciting and non-stop, often brutal at times. There is an array of weapons used in the film, including the double nunchakus that Cheung Lik draws, in one of the fight scenes. Some of the sound extracts used, are taken from the spaghetti western *Once Upon a Time in the West* which adds to the mood. Chen Sing has starred in many other movies, but this one, along with *Bloody Fists*, *Black List* and *Brutal Boxer*, are all time favorites. I have watched this movie on numerous occasions over time, and I am still amazed at the nicely choreographed fight scenes.

I was fortunate enough to see this movie at the cinema in 1973, as a kid growing up in the West Indies. In fact, I went to a cinema to watch it three times over the same weekend. Would have gone more times, had I been given the chance. I remember the shows being sold out on every occasion. Those memories remain with me up to this day. The film was later released with different titles, depending on the format. We anxiously await for it to show up as a Blu-Ray release from the 35mm source. Until then, I recommend viewing the English dubbed version that is in circulation. Excellent stuff!

Duel of Karate 鐵腿降魔 (1970)

DVD Title: To Subdue the Evil

Aka: 鐵沙掌決鬥空手道

Origin: Taiwan

*Cast: Tien Peng, Chen Hung-lieh,
Doris Lung Chun-erh,
Yi Yuan, Huang Chun*

The opening scene starts with a grudge duel between two rivals, where Yi Yuan is defeated by Huang Chun. Three years later, Huang Chun and his wife are having their twin babies tattooed. Yi Yuan makes an appearance with his gang to take revenge. Both parents are killed in during the fight. The baby boys survive, but are separated during a rescue.

Twenty years later, the separated brothers (Tien Peng and Chen Hung-lieh) find themselves on separate sides. Tien Peng has mastered the 'Iron Seal Palm' technique from his adopted teacher, and vows revenge on his murdered parents. Yi Yuan has four skillful Japanese karate fighters who are also involved, that Tien

Peng must get rid of first. Lung Chun-erh plays a table dealer at gambling room, that gets involved with Chen Hung-lieh, who now works for Yi Yuan as his bodyguard. Chen Hung-lieh is tasked with killing Tien Peng's teacher. Afterwards, both brothers meet and get into a fight. Tien Peng is mortally wounded. Both realize that they are brothers, having seeing each others tattoos. Tien Peng tells Chen that Yi Yuan is their parents murderer, before dying. Chen goes after Yi Yuan and gets his revenge.

This was an entertaining movie for its year, with lots of violent fights. Despite the use of wire effects and some hovering, the martial arts action flowed throughout the film. The English voices used in the dubbing may raise a few eyebrows, but overall it's still worth taking a look.

The Black Belt 黑帶仇 (1973)

UK Title: Kung Fu the Head Crusher
US Title: Revenge of the Dragon

Origin: Hong Kong

*Cast: Pai Ying (Yuan Ying),
Fong Yau (Tsao Wei),
Cheung Lik (Yang Shang-cheng),
Sun Lan (Brothel pimp)
Au-Yeung (Judy Juan 'Sally')*

This one opens up with a Karate grading session, where Fong Yau (Tsao Wei) is put through his paces, and leaves the dojo with a certificate. He meets with a couple of his gang and learns that his buddy Cheung Lik (Yang Shang), who had once helped him out during a brawl, was injured in a contest with ex-cop Pai Ying (Yuan Ying). Tsao is aggrieved to hear that his pal Yang had taken a beating, decides to go after Yuan Ying. Tsao ends up at Yuan Ying's yard, but only finds that his mother and blind sister Au-Yeung (Sally), are at home. Tsao rapes the blind sister and strangles the mother with his black belt.

GOLDIG FILMS (H.K.) 協利電影(香港)公司

森張

THE BLACK BELT

導編

Presented by:
ALEX GOUW
Produced by:
HENDRICK GOZALI
Production Manager:
CHAN KING
Martial Art Instructor:
YUEN WO PING
Directed by:
CHEUNG SUM

Starring:
PAK YING CHEUNG LIK FONG YEA

KO YUEN   HELEN MA   AU YEUNG PIU SAN
SAM WOY   KI YUEN   HON KWOK CHOY
CHAN LIN WAI   TAM TIN   LEUNG SIU WAH

The original nerve-shattering sensation

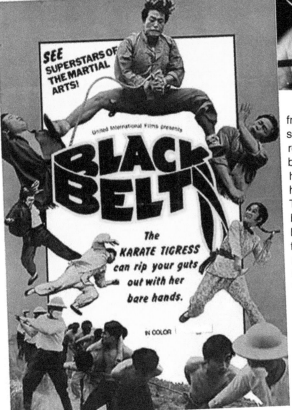

Yuan Ying later returns home from Singapore to find his abused sister, and his dead mother. He reports the incident to the police, but vows to find his mother's killer himself. After getting a tip off, he stumbles on a place where Tsao's lackies are holding a bunch of kidnapped girls, whom he rescues. Later, Sally and a friend overhears Tsao talking at a restaurant. She recognizes his voice, and notifies her brother Yuan.

Yuan chases down and kills 'Cripple', one of Tsao's mates. Tsao is pissed off and plots to get back at Yuan first (marvellous stuff). Yang Shang meets up with his mate Tsao, but dislikes his crooked business, and so decides to rescue Sally who is also captured. Tsao tries to run off with the kidnapped birds, but Yuan is about and they end up fighting, until the police arrive to stop Yuan from killing Tsao.

Proper '70s 'no holds barred' basher, with Pai Ying and Cheung Lik displaying some solid boot work. Added, is Sun Lan in his regular 'skinny guy' role. Yuen Wah even makes an appearance as a thug. The punch and block sound effects, with snippets of some cool music, creates a nice vibe for the film to flow. The lyrics used in the English dub is excellent, and as always, makes for easy viewing. With some decent acting, from a pretty good cast, this is highly recommended. Niceness!

Five SHAOLIN MASTER Collectors

by Alan Donkin

Welcome to the second part of the feature on kung fu movie poster collectors. Or, as Shakespeare famously put it: The Triumph of Kung Fu Arts, Part 3, Act 2, Scene It All Before. Except, you haven't. The questions may be the same, but the answers are as wide and varied as those of the first part. Five different collectors, based in five different countries. Some commonalities, but many deviations of experience. It's been an absolute joy to pull together, and I hope you enjoy reading their recollections and thoughts as much as I have.

James Marshall

James is a Bristolian currently living in Thailand. He has a vast collection of posters, lobby cards, photographs and movies. He is the owner of The Marshall Archive of Asian films on social media, where there are a variety of items available for sale or trade, so that he can fund the acquisition of new items for the archive. He also has a YouTube channel dedicated to his quest to further his collection. He is currently authoring a comprehensive guide to Thai cinema, which he hopes to release in the near future.

AD: *How did you get into collecting posters, and how do you source them?*

JM: I've always had an addictive personality. When I was young, I started with foreign coins, then collected *Star Wars* merchandise. My interests were re-aligned late in 1994, age fourteen, when I borrowed some of Jackie Chan's Lo Wei films from a friend. I then bought the first film in my own collection, an *Operation Condor* ex-rental, released by Entertainment Video.

Dragon Fist, *Police Story 2* and *3*, and *Drunken Master* soon followed, and I became a die-hard Jackie Chan fan, which soon spawned into an all-encompassing love of HK cinema. I started out collecting old second-hand tapes from car boot sales and ex-rentals, as well as new releases from Eastern Heroes, M.I.A. and Made In Hong Kong, who were just starting to become popular. I was in the right place at the right time, luckily for me.

I didn't really start collecting posters until a few years later, because I was a school kid with little money, and there just wasn't anything around. It began with Hollywood films like *Lethal Weapon 4*, *The Big Hit*, *Shanghai Noon*, *Tomorrow Never Dies* and *Maximum Risk*, where Asian stars and directors tried to cross over. I got some rental versions for free from the rental shops, and in the late 90s I started getting posters from cinemas, as well as some direct from the distributors, like *First Strike* and *Corruptor*. There were also some shops that sold reproductions, like Athena, where I got *The Big Boss*, and Forbidden Planet. There was also an indie shop in Bristol called Global Collectables where I got a few press books and press kits, and my *Tomorrow Never Dies* poster with the wrong spelling.

In 1996 I went to the Eastern Heroes event in London and met Jet Li. I soon realised that all roads lead to London, and started to save money to make visits there a few times a year. It started with Chinatown, which had three shops that had movie stuff. One, whose name escapes me, had VCDs. The second, Bernard Seven, sold VCDs and A4 flyers for new releases. The third, Jensen's, stocked VCDs, some Malay VHS tapes, and later, to my annoyance, I found out that they also had posters for new releases, but you had to ask for them. I got a LOT of posters from them after I found out (though it's sad to think what I missed out on prior to this revelation). I also found a few second-hand video places round London.

Later on, I saw an advert in a magazine for 'movie days' at Westminster Central Hall, which was a large merchandise fayre. It included a number of sellers from Europe who brought French and Italian posters with them, including one of my favourites, the enormous French grande for *Thundering Mantis* (1980). There was also the Electric Ballroom in Camden that had a similar, but smaller, event with mostly UK sellers. One day at the Ballroom I was lucky enough to meet Toby by accident and this time got a chance to talk to him, and it turned out he had a market stall just up the road at Camden Lock. My sister (luckily for me) lives in Essex, and is just off the end of the underground, so I started staying with her and extending my stays to two or three days, instead of day trips. I would visit one of the two fayres, Chinatown, and Toby and his gang, who were always there, including Rodney Dennis, Chris Mercer and Andy Smith. John Brennan, who worked for Eastern Heroes, was living very close to my sister in Wood Green, so I would go and see him in the evenings, and traded many items from him. I got my first *Cinemart* magazines this way (I love that magazine so much!).

One day in 2002 when I was with Toby, his friend Bill Bennett came over, clutching a load of posters from Thailand that he'd brought back from holiday. I bought four of them from him, including *Yes, Madam* (1985), *Holy Virgin vs The Evil Dead* (1991) and *Zu Warriors* (1983). It was love at first sight! He had so many I wanted, and I had little money, so I tried very hard to find a source to buy more from at a lower price. Internet auctions were starting to become big and a number of Thai sellers were using

them. I found a couple who sold movie stuff and spoke English, and started telling them what I wanted and asking them to show me what they could get. They got me a lot of good things and sometimes they had HK versions too. I got my first Shaw Brothers posters from them! This formed the backbone of my Shaw Brothers poster collection, which now totals around 370 (one day I will have them all!). There were also websites where I would tease myself by looking at all the HK versions I wanted. The House that Mac Built and Twinkle in HK received regular visits, but Mac was for show only, and Twinkle was very expensive. I traded a load of *Chungking Express* UK posters from ICA for some stuff I wanted from Twinkle, but most of what I got is not worth anywhere near what those *Chungking* posters are worth today. Sadly, I did not even keep one for myself.

In 2007, my mother decided to kick me out of the house and I had to go somewhere. I had managed to save some money and decided to take the opportunity to relocate to Asia. HK was the dream, but much too expensive, and I ended up in Thailand. Mostly for economic reasons, but the posters definitely factored into that decision. Paul Fonoroff, who I knew because he let me publish his film reviews in my short-lived *Oriental Film Review* magazine, said: "Thailand has a lot of HK materials there, I got loads from markets". So, I decided to try my luck, and I have, thankfully, had many opportunities here to increase my HK magazine, poster and lobby card collections, while also starting my Thai collection, although those opportunities are fewer and farther between these days. I also have Korean, Japanese and Indonesian collections, but they are a lot smaller. Things were a lot better back then than they are now, and I have managed to buy thousands of posters here over the last fourteen years. Many were from street sellers, and I've secured some amazing hauls.

AD: *Have you experienced any differences in the ease of sourcing them over the years?*
JM: Yes. For a start, prices have risen (a lot!) and there is a lot less of it around. Many sellers have given up, as the money involved was not good. Thailand's government has cracked down on some

local street markets, deeming them illegal, so some good sources were cut off. Now, there are a lot of new sellers, mostly only selling on the internet, but they do not have anything I want, or their prices are a lot higher. From 2007 until maybe 2012 were the good times – with a lot of stuff at relatively low prices. These days I see people trying to sell posters for ten times what I paid back then. It's amazing and sad, the changes that have happened here since. I had some amazing days back then, with large hauls of new bits I could barely carry, but now I have most of what I see, and buy a lot less. Now I mostly import from other countries again. I have thought about moving elsewhere to try my luck, but moving the collection around is awkward and expensive, so I will probably stay here.

AD: *Why do you collect posters?*
JM: Because I love the films, because I love the art, because it makes me happy, because I love putting the pieces of the puzzle together, because it gives me a reason to get up every day. I am very much a completist and hope to have it all some day. I know I never can, but that doesn't stop me from trying! My interests aren't limited to kung fu posters. I have films and materials from films of every genre. If I don't have it and the price is right, I get it. I have a thirst for knowledge, and part of what I love about this is finding out about 'lost' films that nobody has. Often, there is no mention of them on the internet at all. No entries in books, just the residual evidence that they once existed – like an old

magazine article, some photos, a poster. They deserve to be documented so that they are not forgotten. Just this week, I got a lobby set from a film that is only available in poor quality, and some cards from a lost film that is known to exist, but I can find no mention of it anywhere. This love of material linked to rare films is long-standing. Even in the early days at the Westminster show, seeing posters of rare films, or Shaws that were unavailable at the time, was reassuring. It was tangible evidence that these films did exist and were out there. To this day, I still get that thrill when I find a rare poster for a film that is either

unknown, or stubbornly lost. At the moment I have about 12,000 posters, 15,000 lobby cards and 8,000 items of physical media. It always will continue to grow until I die. One day, I'd like to see a huge database

of every film ever made, fully accessible online and available to watch, including images of the theatrical poster, lobbies and photographs. I know that's not very likely, but it would be nice. Trying to find material for obscure films is a real labour of love. It's also very educational.

AD: Which are your favourite posters, and why?
JM: My primary fondness is for Thai posters. Don't get me wrong – there's some amazing posters from Hong Kong, Japan, Taiwan and Korea. However, there's something unique about the Thai variants from the 1960s to the 1980s. Every country is different, and some are good and some are bad. I have favourites from all over the world, but the Thai versions have more consistently amazing artwork. The majority of HK/Taiwan films from the '60s to the '80s seem to have been released in Thai

cinemas, and had art posters that were usually great. Sadly, they stopped doing the artwork posters in the 1990s, and most posters since have been boring photo montages, or the American version with Thai writing placed on it.

AD: Any regrets?
JM: Money! Or lack of it! Whenever I get some money, I always try to keep some saved, especially for those moments when something good turns up. It really sucks when you want something so badly, but you can't afford it, because you must pay the rent. I have missed out on many good things that way. I have had a few bad experiences with bad people who borrow things and do not return them, so I never lend things any more. A few items have gotten wet by accident, or ripped, and I always regret that. My Spanish *Enter The Fat Dragon* poster suffered a big rip in it

one day when something got dropped. I need to find another one! I always try to replace things that get damaged, but it is not always possible. These items are hard to store and take care of well. Whilst government film archives have large budgets to buy space and materials, I am limited to money I earn, and my room. I hope one day to have some sort of facility to store things properly. There are too many secrets hidden and languishing in film archives that we have no access to. We collectors and addicts need to band together to keep the light shining on those lost gems, and help search for them. There are many experts across the world who know things that few people know, and they need to be in the right places at the right times to find these hidden treasures. I have made a few pretty major discoveries whilst here, such as the Thai films featuring Wilson Tong and Lee Yi Min, the different Thai version of *Jungle Heat*, and other stuff. I hope one day that every film can easily be available for anyone who wants to see it. Meanwhile, the research continues.

Markus Popella

Markus is a collector based in Bochum, Germany. He has been collecting material related to Bruce Lee for more than 30 years, but only cast the net wider to include posters and lobbies featuring other films and stars a decade ago.

MP: I started out collecting only Bruce Lee stuff. This was mainly magazines and books at first. Later, I sought Bruce Lee posters and lobby cards. Slowly, this expanded into Jackie Chan memorabilia, then Bruceploitation stuff. Eventually my collecting interests grew to encompass all martial arts films. Usually, I prefer lobby cards, because they show more scenes from the film, and they are easier to store. However, I also love posters, because some of them are beautifully painted and designed.

Back in the day, I was lucky enough to find a collector who was about to sell lots of his stuff. Over the years I bought a lot of material from him. Some of it I already had, but I take the doubles anyway, because

I can either sell it, or trade it for things I don't have. Sometimes I find nice posters on e-Bay, but over the years it has become

more and more difficult to find them. If possible, I prefer to acquire mint condition posters. However, used is okay too!

AD: *Which are your favourite posters, and why?*

MP: I like the HK and Taiwanese originals, but there's a lot of love to be found in some of the German variants. I particularly like the original Shaw Brothers pieces for *Vengeance!* (1970), *Pursuit of Vengeance* (1977) and *Ten Tigers of Kwangtung* (1979). Some of the German posters I love are *Four Real Friends* (1974), *The Mar's Villa* (1977) and *Fatal Strike* (1974). There's some really nice original imagery on them, or they use exciting designs for the posters and tweak them.

AD: *Which are your least favourite posters, and why?*

MP: I hate ridiculous drawings. They really break the immersion and just look embarrassingly amateurish. The posters for *Karato, Funf Todliche Finger* (1971) spring to mind.

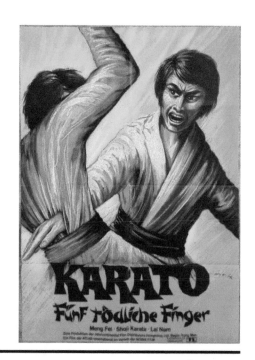

Ryo Sato

Ryo is a collector based in Tokyo, Japan. He is twenty-eight years old. He has lived Hong Kong and Taiwanese action movies since he was little. He has an excellent collection of videos, DVDs, posters, press books and lobby cards. He used to work in the movie industry, with stuntmen from the Japan Action Club, founded by Sonny Chiba. He later moved into the video industry, remastering old movies and repairing films.

AD: *Why do you collect posters?*

RS: Old kung fu movie posters from Hong Kong and Japan are attractive in design. The written characters and illustrations are powerful and attract the viewers' interest. It's not all about the aesthetics, though. There's another reason I collect. We Japanese love Hong Kong movies. Both older and younger people who share my hobby mainly like Bruce Lee, Jackie Chan, Jet Li and Donnie Yen. I also love great action stars such as Tan Tao-liang, Bruce Le, Dragon Lee, Alexander Lo Rei, Robert Tai, Simon Lee, John Liu and Billy Chong. These are less well-known, but I like them. I love their acting and their action sequences. So, I use social media to publish my collection of posters featuring these stars. This raises awareness of them and is my way of telling them how great they are!

AD: *How do you source them?*

RS: My primary sources were Japanese

auction sites. I also use SNS (social networking services) to buy and trade with people all over the world.

AD: *Have you experienced any difficulties in sourcing posters over the years?*

RS: I have only collected posters in earnest for six or seven years. It was hard at first. Most people in Japan can't speak English because their education in the language is not good. For the posters I wanted, I had to ask a Japanese import agency, but it was very expensive. At that time, I was just into my early twenties and didn't have much money. It is only recently that my poster collection has started to gather pace and expand. It has been assisted by overseas auctions and trading

with collectors using English translation apps.

AD: *Which are your favourite posters, and why?*

RS: There are many! Carter Wong's *Killer of Snake, Fox of Shaolin's* (1979) international poster is a good one. Dragon

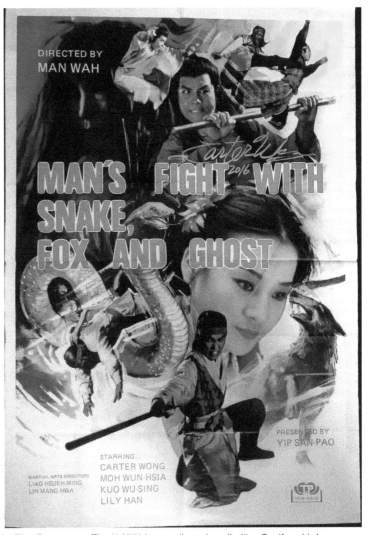

Lee's *The Dragon on Fire* (1978) is excellent. I really like Godfrey Ho's *Mission Thunderbolt* (1983). Oshima Yukari's *Angel's Mission* (1989) is excellent. Alexander Lou's *Ninja: The Final Duel* (1986) is fabulous. These posters are my treasures. Some were signed by Carter Wong, Godfrey Ho and Toby Russell.

AD: Which are your least favourite posters, and why?
RS: I don't have any!

AD: Do you prefer mint or well-worn copies?
RS: I like the posters where you can feel the history in your hands. A thumb tack mark or a fold can prove authenticity.

AD: Have you ever found a bargain?
RS: Yes. The Taiwanese poster of Sonny Chiba and Nora Miao's *Tokyo-Seoul-Bangkok Drug Triangle* (1973). I sourced it from a Taiwanese auction. I have framed it!

AD: Ever missed out on one?
RS: Yes! The original HK poster for the Indonesian kung fu film *Cobra* (1977).

AD: Do you have any regrets about collecting?
RS: There are many – usually when the poster I wanted was bought by another collector.

Mike Leeder

Mike is a casting director, producer and actor based in Hong Kong. That's not all. He is a regular contributor to magazines and blu-ray special features on Asian cinema. Check out his imdb listings. This guy has more credits than a hacked arcade machine. He lives and breathes Eastern movies.

AD: *Why do you collect posters, and how did you get into collecting them?*

ML: Back when dinosaurs ruled the Earth and I first started getting into loving movies of various genres, including kung fu and Hong Kong movies, we didn't have Blu-Ray or DVD, or even VHS back then. So, often the only way to remember a movie was to collect things associated with it, like novelizations of the movie or TV show, or posters if you could get them. I had *Star Wars*, *Doctor Who*, *The Professionals*, etc, mixed in with a big quad *Enter the Dragon* (1973) poster. Then someone gave me a couple of Jackie Chan ones, and I just started collecting. And I have kept it up to this day! My bedroom back in England still has some classic posters, including signed ones by Jackie Chan, Cynthia Rothrock and Van Damme, that I really should bring over to Hong Kong. There's loads in my house here, and more in storage at my office.

AD: *How do you source them, and have you experienced any difficulties in sourcing them over the years?*

ML: It was actually easier to get posters in the UK, America and Europe! You could get them at collectors' markets, movie memorabilia shops, and from people like Ricky Baker and Chris Alexis. Sometimes I'd buy them 'coz I love that particular movie, and sometimes just 'coz the posters for a particular film were beautiful or really cool. Or sometimes really mad! When I came to Hong Kong, I did think that HK movie memorabilia would be quite easy to find. It was a hell of an eye-opener when I arrived in 1990 to discover that there was no sell-through market, and cinemas were reluctant to part with posters and stuff. That's where being a writer always helped, as I could get posters and lobby cards for articles and stuff. In the early '90s they would also fly-post HK movie posters everywhere, and if you timed it right, you could either get the guys to give you a poster or two, or give them a few bucks, or, in the worst case scenario, take them down yourself! And yes, I will admit to going up to huge bus shelters a few times with an Allen-key, and opening them up to get a particular poster I wanted!

These days, there's a few collectors in

Hong Kong who have some great collections and are willing to sell or trade, and thanks to e-Bay, etc, you can often find some good stuff online. About three years ago, some guys opened up a movie memorabilia store in Mong Kok, which for the few months it was open had some great stuff. I traded with the owners and even gave them a few for free, and vice versa. But rental costs, and in HK, a lack of customers, saw it closing after a few months.

AD: *What are you favourite and least favourite posters? Why?*

ML: That's a hard one. The *Eastern Condors* (1987) line-up poster, the *Dragons Forever* (1988) original HK release, the 1998 *Black Eagle* poster (as both Van Damme and Sho Kosugi signed it for me), the Korean cinema poster for *Shiri* (1999), and the *Drunken Master* (1978) poster that I got Jackie, Hwang Jang-lee, Roy Horan, Ng See-yuen and Yuen Woo-ping to sign, which I'm getting framed at the moment.

There's so many I love. Outside of kung fu films, I love the original UK Quads for *Star Wars*, *Highlander*, etc. I go through phases, so I do end up swapping posters over quite frequently. There's a huge bus shelter poster I have for a HK comedy film – *Tom, Dick and Hairy* (1993) – which I love. It's a great, fun design, and I got all the cast and director, etc, to sign it. My least favourite? A few movies I've been in, where I've seen the posters and gone: "What???????"

AD: *Do you prefer mint copies or copies that have good signs of age? Do you have any regrets?*

ML: I've got some that are mint that look fantastic, but others that are mint can look too fresh. The slightly-worn, slightly-aged ones are my favourites.

AD: *Have you ever chanced upon a bargain?*

ML: There have been some great, lucky acquisitions! A friend of mine was a sales agent, and when she closed, she let me go in and just raid her poster library from 1990-2015. I got some great ones – all for the price of a bottle of wine! Then there's been the expensive misses. There used to be a HK magazine, called *Cinemart*. When the owner, Alpha Lau, closed the doors, he threw the majority of his stuff in a skip. He then called me, but by the time I got there, HK was having a black rainstorm. It was heart-breaking to see so many rare posters, lobbycards, and photos just ruined by the rain. What's funny in this hobby is that fans of the movies aren't the only collectors. I've had some instances where, when I've acquired a rare poster, and wanted to get it signed by the actor/director, they've said, "I've not got this one!" I bought a whole bunch of Bruce Le posters, as he's a friend, and I wanted him to sign them the next time he was in HK. I went to meet him and I left with one signed poster. He left with twenty, that now hang in his office in Beijing!

One of my biggest regrets related to a friend of mine. His family owned a cinema in Kowloon City, and when they closed it, his dad kept telling me he would let me take all the posters and lobbycards I wanted. This cinema had been open during late '70s to mid '90s, and I knew that they had some good ones. I had to go to China for a shoot, which got delayed, and by time I got back, his dad had thrown everything out. That is the treasure trove that got away!

Jared King

Jared works for the Old Bill Stateside. When he's not filming Police Story 8: USA, *he's upsetting film fans throughout the world with his fortnightly 'OK' pocket reviews on social media. He is married to his hobby. He also has a wife, a son, and a daughter.*

AD: *Why do you collect posters?*

JK: I collect posters because I am a rather huge fan of Hong Kong cinema. These are the only posters I collect, along with lobby cards, and the films themselves in any format I can find.

AD: *How did you get into collecting posters?*

JK: I started to follow Hong Kong cinema in 1997. Not much was available in the video stores in my area. When the films began to enjoy a more widespread release via Tai Seng, a few would show up at local video stores where I began to rent anything I could get my hands on. Around this time, the US versions of Jackie and Jet films were also released and, as I was friendly with the video store clerks in my area, once they were finished displaying those posters, they put them aside for me. So, I had the US versions of *Rumble in the Bronx* (1995) and *Twin Warriors* (*Tai Chi Master* – 1993) adorning my walls. Video stores in our local mall – Suncoast Video and Saturday Matinee – had a few posters that I picked up as well. There was a cool variant of John Woo's *The Killer* (1989), that I think I may still have. I started off by collecting the films themselves. This was just before the internet boom and e-Bay. A few years later, e-Bay sprang up, and it was easier to find additional Hong Kong film ephemera, other than just the films themselves.

AD: *How do you source them?*

JK: Mainly e-Bay. I have grown to know a bunch of sellers throughout the years who I can safely deal with. Either buying or trading. The online Hong Kong poster/lobby card friends I have made are really fantastic people to deal with. I visited Hong Kong nine years ago and a few sellers that I had been dealing with lived there. I had purchased a bunch of posters from a few of the dealers, and instead of having them ship them to me, I figured I would pick them up myself since I was going to be in town. And they were all more than accommodating. One dealer dropped off a

tube of posters at my hotel while I was out sight-seeing. Another made the trip to my hotel. Once there, he popped the trunk of his car open to reveal a treasure trove of posters and lobby cards, so we wound up on the street for two hours wheelin' and dealin'. He spoke no English and I don't speak Cantonese. But he went home a few hundred bucks richer, and I had a trunk load of new posters I had to buy a new suitcase for. Yet another guy, who has become a really good social media buddy, visited me at my hotel with posters and other movie goodies in tow for me. A long-time dealer I had been buying from for forever even opened up his office to me on a Sunday evening so I could pick up a bunch of prints. Everyone I have dealt with in Hong Kong has been exceptionally gracious. Especially on that trip. And then there was a Hong Kong film director who invited my wife and I out for drinks, and showed up with the poster for his new film

just for me. So, yeah. I have lived a charmed Hong Kong movie poster collecting life. LOL!

AD: *Have you experienced any differences in the ease of sourcing them over the years?*

JK: I have noticed that collecting Hong Kong film ephemera, whether it be films, posters, or lobby cards, comes in fits and starts. The buying/trading landscape can be barren for a while, and then all of a sudden a bunch of titles pop up out of nowhere. I figure this tends to happen because I have so many posters. Maybe the ones that are popping up during a 'barren' period, I may already have. So, I just see the landscape as less than fruitful.

AD: *Which are your favourite posters, and why?*

JK: This is a tough question. Like, which is your favourite child? While it's not a *Sophie's Choice* decision, I kinda lean toward the posters of the Hong Kong film era that I am in love with: the late '80s to mid '90s. So, posters like John Woo's *Hard*

Boiled (1992) and Ringo Lam's *City on Fire* (1987) are the ones that I enjoy the most. Particularly *City on Fire*, as a few years back I was able to meet Ringo, and he autographed the poster, amongst a few others. I also really dig a few of the CAT III posters that I have.

My faves are the two *Dr. Lamb* (1992) prints I have, and my two *Run and Kill* (1993) prints. All four are behind glass, with the two *Dr. Lamb* ones actually hanging up in one of the rooms in my home. Much to the dismay of my wife.

Those two films are faves of mine, and both were directed by one of my all-time fave directors, the late, great Billy Tang. I also have another Billy Tang film poster framed and hanging up in the same room, the *Young and Dangerous* (1996) knock-off, *Street of Fury* (1996), which is an underappreciated gem of a film, and better than *Y&D*. In my opinion of course. And it's a fantastic-looking poster. I also just got in the poster to the film *Bio-Cops* (2000), and it's another super-fun stunner that I would like to frame.

AD: *Which are your least favourite posters, and why?*
JK: I have a bunch of Thai posters of Hong Kong films, and while they look quite wonderful, and the artistry is a lot of fun to look at, they don't hold a comfy place in my heart. I have a thing that I only want or like the film poster from the specific country the film is from. If the film is from Hong Kong, then I must have the Hong Kong poster. If the film is from Taiwan, then the poster must be the Taiwanese version. It's an odd, maybe snobbish, thing, but it's something that lives in me.

AD: *What else do you like about them?*
JK: I like that they are a snapshot of a particular time in Hong Kong cinema history. Each era has a format for posters. The ones that I drool over are from the '80s and '90s.

AD: *Do you prefer mint copies or copies that have good signs of age? Why?*
JK: This is a great question. I have always preferred a used and abused poster. Especially when I know that it may have been hanging up in a movie theatre during the film's initial

run. Now, of course, I would prefer for the poster not to look like it was used as a wee-wee pad for a bulldog. But cracks, creases, pinholes and tape marks are more than welcome in my collection. It gives the poster a rich history. Heck, even if the poster was just hanging up in some dude's bedroom and never saw the lights of a theatre lobby, that's enough history for me. Someone enjoyed it enough to pin or tape it up on their wall. I can relate. That used to be me. And that's cool.

AD: *Have you ever chanced upon a bargain?*
JK: Oh boy. Once I was Googling yard sales and garage sales. And up popped a listing for someone selling about five-hundred Hong Kong movie posters, but by pick-up only. No shipping. Ok. No big deal. I have done the pick-up thing before.

Further investigation found that the seller lived in Canada. Well, I'm in New York. Five-hundred plus miles away. My wheels began to turn, and I started planning what I would say to my wife for her to let me go to Canada for these posters. I came up with the idea of bringing her along, and making it a long holiday weekend for us.

So, after emailing the seller back and forth, discovering he was mutual friends with other social media friends and vetting the reliability of him, and making sure I wasn't walking into a face-to-face with a serial killer, my wife and I drove the thousand plus miles round trip to pick up the five-hundred posters, plus a few other Hong Kong film collectibles. All for the princely sum of... $1,000US! $2 a poster! I still can't believe it. Best vacay ever, man. Over the next year or so, the seller also unloaded a shit-ton of full and half sets of lobby cards on me for around another grand.

AD: *Any regrets?*

JK: Oh, man. I've spent tens of thousands of dollars on all of my Hong Kong memorabilia nonsense. Money that could have gone on a better car. A better home. Worldly vacations with my wife. Money I could have put away for retirement. Put into stocks. Tucked away for my children's education. Or just ease my paycheck-to-paycheck existence. So, do I have any regrets? Not at all.

DEVIL HUNTERS

Intermission

And there we have it. Another five great collectors, with their unique tales and takes on the hobby. I originally envisaged this as a two-parter, but the response has been tremendous, so I'm happy to present the third and final part in the next issue.

EASTERN HEROES Hall of Fame
SPARTA EDITION

by Scott Adkins

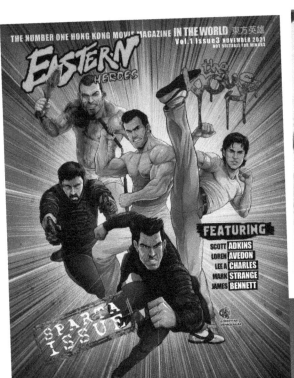

Eastern Heroes has been a supporter of Hong Kong Cinema since it was first produced back in 1989. But with the new re-launch of the magazine, I feel we can explore action cinema in a broader sense, giving coverage to more local home grown talent both here in the UK and the U.S.A.

For issue 3, I interviewed five established and also up-and-coming martial action movie stars who I am privileged to know and have watch their careers bloom from the '80s until the present day. The cover has been greeted with much success, with me getting many messages that this could be turned into a great action flick just based on the superb imagery created by the talented duo Shaolin Jaa and CrikeArt99.

Welcome to the section I have called the Sparta section.

Loren Avedon

"Of course, my all-time favourite is the original, the one and only, Bruce Lee."

Loren will be no stranger to people of a certain 'vintage' who enjoyed dining on the action menu of their local video store. Oldies like me, basically. I lost count of the amount of times I sat with my dear old mum on the sofa and watched the wonderful Avedon duo: *No Retreat, No Surrender 2*, and *The King of the Kickboxers*. Back in the day, Loren visited the UK with Vincent Lyn. He attended an exhibition in Birmingham 'Clash of the Titans' organised by *Martial Arts Illustrated*. As always, my mum was helping me out with a stall and chatting up the local talent. Once she knew that Loren was there, she made a bee-line for him, and I'm sure there was a kiss involved. At the stage, I wondered if this superstar was being lined up to be my future stepdad!

Loren was, of course, a perfect gentleman towards my mum. He is a very humble, lovely person. He had gained experience in front of the camera from a young age, starring in commercials at the age of five. Following some television appearances, he gained worldwide recognition in the aforementioned two films, plus *No Retreat, No Surrender 3: Blood Brothers*.

Loren is a very accomplished martial artist, achieving the rank of fifth degree black belt in taekwondo. He is looking to return to the action movie scene, and recent talks with other stars on our front cover have suggested a potential collaboration is on the cards. We can but hope! I caught up with him recently and asked the honoured addition to the *Eastern Heroes* Hall of Fame a few questions.

SA: How old were you when you started martial arts?
LA: I had tried many different classes at Beverly High after school and at Roxbury Park in Beverly Hills at the rec centre during high school but found only sadistic unprofessional instructors that had no real teaching skills. Basically, it was the non-art of fighting and getting hurt, with no structure. After I graduated High School and was almost eighteen, I visited Jun Chong Tae Kwon Do, a tae kwon do/hap ki do school that also stressed boxing skills and weapons, that a couple friends of mine were members of and finally found Master Jun Chong, Masters Phillip and Simon Rhee, and great instructors like Peter Malota (Luljerai) at Jun Chong Tae Kwon Do. That's when I began my real martial arts Training.

SA: Growing up, who were your influences and what movies inspired you to take up becoming an action movie star.
LA: My first influence was the immortal Bruce Lee. It was 1973 and I was a boy of eleven years old when my friend and adopted big brother Tyler McKenzie (Fred Astaire's Grandson) took me to a movie

theater in Bath England to see *Fists of Fury* sometimes called *The Chinese Connection*. It was rated 'X' and I was nowhere near seventeen quite obviously. The timid ticket booth lady forked over the ticket after Tyler left me to fend for myself. I remember acknowledging her terse but accurate observation… "You're not seventeen" she said. My steadfast reply was "give me the ticket!" and obviously she did. I left that theater in awe… thinking "I want to be just like him… he doesn't need anybody, and he is so incredibly skilled, powerful, fast and confident… I want to be just like him…"

Sadly about 3 months later my hero was dead. After my return to the States I couldn't get enough of *Kung Fu Theater* onTV and would go to China Town and Monterey Park, Hollywood or downtown LA when there might be a showing of a kung fu movie". I didn't care about the poor dubbing or overacting, I was fascinated by the martial arts fights, and the clearly incredible athletic abilities of the actor/martial artists and the brave stunt men and women. Cannon Films put out some

Chuck Norris movies and some others were making karate movies, but no one came close to Bruce Lee. I remember seeing *Billy Jack* and loving the line "I'm going to take my right foot and wop you on this side of your face… and you want to know something… there's not a damn thing you're gonna be able to do about it".

SA: you're in great shape still very flexible, what is your current training regime?
LA: At fifty-nine I train very low impact and mostly barefoot at the beach or wearing light Adidas TKD shoes. I do most of my training by myself. I do a lot of stretching, breathing exercises, and practice technique with as perfect form as possible. I do a lot of Pomsae (Kata) I have a weight set in my back patio and do what I call super sets. I'll use light weight and do high reps with perfect form. Military press, bent over rows, and bicep curls, all in one set (fifteen to twenty reps of each totaling max sixty every set) with perfect form and breathing, moving from one exercise to the next before I put the bar down. Then I'll do a different three exercise combo. I do a lot of isometrics and plyometrics. I have a litany of injuries that occurred mostly from pushing myself past my physical limits when I was a younger man, and from hitting the ground or being hit. I won't go into all that I have endured as all great athletes eventually pay the price. Fighting for film and in the Dojang back in the day we used very little protection. Tae kwon do and hap ki do demand that you hit the ground. That takes a toll. After forty years I have great muscle memory and have adapted to my age. I have nothing to prove, but I remain supple because that is the most important thing. I can explode for a brief period, but my goals are simple. Keep moving, and maintain my posture, my health and my form, and the warrior mind set. I exercise when I walk, when I sit, with every breath. I have lost some speed but the last thing one loses is Power. I still train with some weapons, but having broken my right wrist five times, there are some things I can't do anymore. Its mind over matter… if you don't

mind, it don't matter. It's about Ki energy and discipline. Good habits, humility, and selflessness. There is more pain as I age but with my experience and knowledge, I feel good, because I choose to. I try to never stop learning, for the mind is the most important thing to keep in shape. Everyone, every second, must master himself, and time is the master of us all. "Be water my friends."

SA: I heard a great story, when you fell ill on the set of No Retreat No Surrender 2 *and Hwang Jang-lee took care of you, please tell the readers about this and your respect for him.*
LA: I love Hwang Jang-lee. He trained me when I first came to Thailand before we began shooting *NRNSII, Raging Thunder*. We met at the gym in the Ambassador Hotel in Bangkok. He was and is soooo powerful, and he made technique look so smooth. As we spent days together on and off the set, he saw how hard I was trying, how much I wanted to do well.

He would joke with me: "You shooting today?" and he would smile. My reply: "Yep, you shooting today?". And he would answer me, with a head shake or a nod, and we would smile. He was playing a part in an English-speaking film and that part was as a bad guy and the only real fight he had in the film was with with Cynthia Rothrock, so he had a lot of down time. He always was so humble and nice but the Chinese stunt men were deathly afraid of him. I remember one scene where a stunt man was to hold his foot as he had caught it as part of the fight. Hwang's next move was to execute a difficult aerial side kick swinging his leg over the top of the other caught foot to throw the side kick, but the stunt man let go of his foot as Hwang was trying to execute that extremely difficult jump up and over in order to kick the man in the chest and for Hwang to land on his feet. Well, when the stuntman let go, Hwang hit the ground hard and got up right away and brushed himself off.

Not a word was said. Complete silence. It was an 'Oh, shit' moment. So, they reset for take two, but before rolling Yuen Kuai had chastised this stunt man. The stunt man was now going to get it. Hwang hit him so hard in the air with that side kick, that it looked like his shoulders almost touched each other as he flew backwards to the ground as Hwang landed gracefully. Yuen Kuai yelled "Cut!" and Hwang looked over to me and raised his eyebrows and smiled. This was my first starring role, so even though I could be off somewhere resting, I was on set watching, soaking everything up like a sponge. One day, I had eaten something that had me throwing up and in the outhouse all day on set. They took me to a clinic somewhere in the jungle, as we were in the middle of God knows where. When I was transported to the clinic, I was with the wardrobe lady who spoke perfect English and Thai.

They gave me a couple bags of an IV saline glucose solution and said I had food poisoning,

Hand to hand combat at its most lethal...!

and if I didn't rest for a few days I could die. Hwang was very concerned. He was always helping me, using pressure points, asking me if I was ok, and being like a father, or big brother to me on the set and off. We ate together a lot and kept each other company. So, the production had to shut down for a few days while I recuperated. The Thai crew were so kind, they were always nearby during that time, and so was Hwang. He would come to my room and just sit with me. I guess they could all see I was pretty sick. A few days later I came down to the restaurant where we would go to eat in Saraburi pretty regularly. Hwang went with me for my first real meal. He asked me... "What did you eat that made you sick?" I answered; "American fried rice"... he waved over the waiter and said; "Give me American fried rice" the waiter nodded his head and walked away. Hwang smile at me and said, "I get sick too...". I sat with him and I ate plain rice, soup broth, and some 'mountain chicken'. A whole chicken on a vertical spit that you could eat with your hands. We shared the Chicken, and he ate every grain of that rice, and we walked back to the hotel. Needless to say, I survived, and was back to work the next day.

After NRNSII, Raging Thunder wrapped I went with Hwang to Taiwan to be with him while he worked on a period piece filmed at Taroko Gorge in Hualien. I watched Hwang wearing in a period piece costume a long-haired wig.

turgutart

He looked so regal riding a beautiful all brown Chinese horse followed by a cast of hundreds of costumed soldiers. We also went to Korea together, where we were guests of his friends and would go to Hostess bars and we stayed at the Ramada Renaissance Hotel there in Seoul. I went with him to Cheju and stayed at one of the hotels he owned there. Cheju Do island is where so many young Korean married couples go for their honeymoon and just to visit and have pictures made. Hwang took me to the road that is in Korea where you think and feel you are going downhill but the car rolls backwards!? As it came time to go back home, I left Hwang, as he had to continue with his work. I slept on the floor of Cynthia Rothrock and Yuen Biao's apartment as I had no money to afford a hotel and Cynthia was working. I left the next morning for the U.S. After that, Jun Chong had hired Hwang to be in a film that I was to star in L.A. but turned down. I brought him to visit my mom and introduce him, as I had told my mom so much about him. I felt horrible that Hwang was all by himself all the time, but I had gone back to college and was teaching. The last I saw of Hwang was at some hotel in L.A.'s Korea Town. I haven't seen him since, but I see him on IG and know he is still the immortal man who thirty-six years ago had an American son. I hope someday to see him again. Until then he remains in my heart, and in my memory forever.

SA: *One of my all time favourite films is* King of the Kickboxers. *Tell the readers what is was like making that movie.*

LA: As with *Blood Brothers* I was a part of the casting process in LA and was so happy that I would be working with Billy Blanks and Keith Cooke. *KOTKB* was the last of my three-picture deal with Seasonal. I knew it was going to be a tough shoot because we would be in Thailand again and in Hong Kong

and working with Lucas Lo. When I arrived in Bangkok, I was relieved that Tony Leung Shinhong was head of the stunt team and that a few of the guys I had worked with before were there as well. I didn't really know Keith Cooke or Billy at all but as with all the greats, they are and were truly humble. I had been training like an animal because I knew I would be getting the crap beat out of me as my character was meant to be taught a lesson. The hardest of all was the end fight as the Chinese were burning smoke powder to create the haze and I was having a hard time breathing. Not to mention it was 98° Fahrenheit with 95% humidity. Billy and I were so fast that a lot of the fight did not need to be shot a 22fps or 19 to make up for speed. It took two and a half weeks to shoot that final fight, and it was a good thing the hotel in Kanchanpuri was basically a quarter mile from the set. So, every morning we could just walk to work. Billy was so amazing to fight with as he understood instinctively what was necessary and had incredible control. The same with Keith, although both of them knocked the wind out of me several times, not on purpose mind you. I was more worried about the Thai SFX guys rigging dynamite, C4, and diesel fuel and wiring it while we were still working on the set. Same as in *NRNSII, Raging Thunder*. One day I saw an empty box of dynamite near where one the SFX guys was rigging, and he was smoking a cigarette!? Cause of the humidity there was crystal nitro glycerin in the box that had leaked from the dynamite. I said to the Thai SFX guy, "no smoke… boom" gesturing with my arms. "Mai ben lai" he said and took a piece of crystal nitro from the box and touched it to the cherry of his cigarette! It immediately ignited and burned his fingers together.

There were a lot of safety issues as always. Look what just happened on the set of the Alec Baldwin movie here in the US. I have mentioned in other interviews how I would always be pointing out safety issues and they were taken care of. When I got to Hong Kong I met Steve Tartalia, Mark King, and Vincent Lyn on the docks where we shot the opening sequence. We got along great and had a lot of fun after hours shall

we say. I met Michelle Yeoh, and Conan Lee out clubbing. It was great to work with Richard Jaekel, he had a bad hip and could barely walk but he still went with us everywhere, never complained and always was a gentleman. Jerry Trimble had a bit of a chip on his shoulder, he was hitting me full blast on rehearsals, hammer fisted me in the groin just to try and piss me off. He was the 'Golden Boy' of course and I guess thought he should be the star, and was wondering… who the hell is this guy? The only thing he did was upset the stunt team who had grown very protective of me as we had been together for more than three months. You become family. So, they let him have it. Anyway, Jerry and I are friends, we actually used to live on the same street in BH. In enjoyed those few days on the docks of Hong Kong and love it in Thailand. Wherever you work, everyone is part of the team, and always have to look out for each other. *KOTKB* was a great experience. I just feel so grateful to have been a part of the Golden Age of Hong Kong Movies.

SA: What are your thoughts on the current martial arts action movies compared to the movies being made back in the day?
LA: Well, some of the over complex choreo bothers me. I have an eye for detail, I am always finding flaws. It's just the nature of knowing. I guess it's all about what the audience believes. If they are entertained, who am I to say anything. Its also about how they shoot the fights, what the dynamic

is of the character and the film, and what I like to call 'believability', using what is around you and making it organic and then magic can happen. Unless you are playing a superhero, and even then, there has to be an Achilles heel. The human mind needs time to digest the power of the technique, to see and feel the character and the action as an extension of that moment. I hate it when I see stunt men waiting to get into the fight. Or punching so obviously over someone's head. Bruce Lee was so good at having people fly into frame and execute his technique, and in a wide shot have every man in perfect position, moving and acting themselves so as to appear to be finding the moment. Now you can see that in pre-viz and in playback, then there is always take two or however many it takes to get the shot. We didn't have playback, and the choreography was learned and executed on the spot. We had the eyes of the coordinators, cameramen and director, a little power powder, water in the mouth, potters earth and guts. Also there are secrets to throwing blocks, punches and kicks that allow for power and reaction while protecting each other. With the Chinese, the words I will always remember are… "Chuen Bong" which translates to 'Fake'. Which also translates to 'even though you blasted each other, we do another take!' Really what I enjoy seeing, is organic, realistic but heightened action that is unpredictable. Stunt people 'Selling out' as it were. I love the creativity, but if I'm watching a fight and it's been going on for two or three minutes and nobody is out of breath, not sweating, or showing the human side of the moments, then I shake my head. When camera shoots a gaf (a fight), and a lot times these days it's shot on steady cam, rather than with camera on the cameraman's shoulder. Steady cam and that gyro takes power away from any impact. Tight shots to frame out the actor's movement bother me. It's either poor camera work or they are hiding the flaws and not using the full arc of the frame to create power. You lose me at that point. It's hard for me to watch a non-martial artist doing technique. It's so obvious. Now if you get a guy like Keanu Reeves and you put him through a three-month boot camp and have a great stunt team and its 'Gun Fu' mixed with striking, judo, bjj and directed by Chad Stahelski, or JJ Perry and you have John Valera doing choreo… you know they've put in the work and it shows. Sam Hargrave did a great job with *Extraction* and there is a second one in the works I hear. Bottom line, you can do a great fight, but it takes having the right people in all departments. It has to feel dangerous, and sometimes is, and you and the stuntmen/women and partners in the scene that don't mind taking some lumps and they get it on camera and know the editor also knows what he/she is doing, then you've got something. I am so lucky to have learned from the best in the world. To have learned on the job… like Spencer Tracy said… you want to be an actor, audition and work. I think that Scott Adkins is doing a great job, Tony Jaa et al., they're just great to watch. They have something in common, exceptional athletic ability, and they are real martial artists and great human beings. Everybody has an ego, but that doesn't make anything work. You can't fall in love with yourself or complex technique, I want to see realism and power, and I want to be sucked into the moment.

SA: You have a large fan base here in the UK, would you ever consider coming over for an event?
LA: I would love it. I would be honoured. I also have a large fan base in Europe and all over the world. Three generations of fans are out there. There is still a ban on travel due to Covid-19 and variants, but that should change next year.

SA: The new cover has created a lot of response, I could see this being turned into a possible film project with the right script what are your thoughts?
LA: You said it, with the right script we definitely have something worthwhile. I have a great deal of respect for all of the talent on the cover. It all starts with the script. The right script for me involves a character driven story. Necessary and powerful action sequences, realistic but of course creative, with a group of relatable characters with a strong active connection, put into a situation that is very personal (to the characters), creating intriguing and entertaining performances. But there also has to be great work from all production departments. You can't please everyone in an audience, but you can do a damn good job telling a story. If you believe it, the audience will. I suggest we do a talent search to find the next young star(s) of action films as well. I mean why not we'll be casting for other roles as well. For me the importance of any role in a film is to make the movie that's already good on paper,

great on screen. You mentioned someone visiting the set of the latest *Expendables* movie and that the stars weren't speaking to each other and there was a lot of tension and ego on the set. That is so counterproductive and unnecessary. I mean they are already making so much money but can't get along? Says a lot about why 'friendship' in Hollywood or 'Anywood', and all the money in the world comes second to selfishness. Heck, I've fought for things on films, but always with the film and all involved first on my mind, not me. I mean Lucas Lo didn't want to shoot the end of the film *Blood Brothers* where the

brothers reconcile. I put my foot down and demanded that scene be shot. I said, "this is a film about brothers". Lucas said, "Ok, I give you one take" and sure enough its part of the film. People like to work with people who are easy to get along with, instinctively creative, and go above and beyond. As for big budget films, I have no pity for these stars, and their attitude. It's pretty basic, safety first, have fun, work together, get along, 'be it', no 'acting' allowed, (except for fight reactions) and remember two things… 1) You're getting paid to wait and 2) it's just a movie… so help each other make it work. When in doubt cut it out, and trust each other. When there is tension on the set it affects the whole film, it starts with the director and stars/talent and infects the whole group with inspiration or misery. Then God willing in the first case the audience. The camera doesn't lie.

SA: Finally, what plans do you have for the future and congratulations on your recent marriage.

LA: Thank you for the congratulations. Married life is certainly a welcome change and inspiration. I never expected to fall in love again, but then that goes to your first question. The plans I have are always to move forward, in many fields of endeavor. The world has been greatly changed by the pandemic. I feel fortunate that I was able to carry on with my personal life in spite of Covid. My wife is Serbian, one of the few countries that is neutral in Europe. If her country was a part of the EU, I could have never met her family in 2019 and been married in 2020. Overcoming many obstacles requires great inspiration. It's kind of the story of my life, and probably a lot of your readers. Being told I can't do it, or there are great odds against success, has been the majority of my journey. Having obstacles only provides more determination to me and a greater challenge to overcome. It's easy to shrink to the circumstances rather than rise to the occasion. Look at the history of the U.K. and your current adjustment to leaving the E.U. In spite of the difficulty, you remain a great people, and a great nation. I respect all cultures, nations and peoples. No matter their creed, religion, etc. I may not agree with certain ideals, but the only thing I can do is 'be the change I want to see in the world'. I have found in so many cultures, regardless of language that people want to communicate and connect, that people everywhere are very much the same. Everyone wants love, security, appreciation, opportunity, respect and hope. I have never thought I was better than anyone else. So, the future is bright with many possibilities for me. Most importantly, I feel that the best thing that I can do is work as hard as I can to be a good husband, good friend, good father and be as good a person as I can. All the rest is really created by making the space in life for good things to come in, and of course hard work. I have given a lot of my life up to doing the right thing rather than what was easy? I am looking forward and have a lot to look forward to. This period of rebirth for everyone who has been held back and had so much change forced on them is just another opportunity. I pray for those who have been so negatively affected by our times. But I harken back to antiquity, where the greatest moments of human being are created by the worst of conditions. I pray we all come together and stop focusing on what may separate us. When I think I am in control I remember that in reality I have no control over anything. But I do have the choice to be grateful and thankful about how lucky and fortunate I am. I plan to make a difference every day, and whatever comes be thankful.

Lee A. Charles

"From the first time I saw a Bruce Lee movie, I literally became obsessed wanting to be like him."

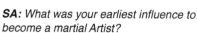

When you meet Lee Charles, you take notice. You may even feel intimidated! He's a big bloke – even a Russian mobster with a private any one would think twice about looking at him the wrong way. Appearances, as they say, can be deceptive. And so it applies to Lee, who is another humble man, without any sense of pretentiousness or ego. I caught up with the lad from Birkenhead recently on the set of *The Expendables 4.*

Lee could have made it in football. As a youngster, he played at various levels for Everton, Tranmere and Wrexham. However, injury curtailed his career, and his contract was terminated. He poured his efforts into martial arts. His interest in that area had been sparked by his childhood love of Bruce Lee films. Unperturbed by his sporting setback, he studied various styles of martial arts and honed his talents. At the time of writing, he is a six-time kickboxing world champion! His route into movies was aided when he trained at the Lee Strasberg Theatre and Film Institute. His martial arts instructor was none other than Benny Urquidez, the famed American kickboxer and screen fighter.

Lee has appeared in many productions over the years. His most notable recent credit was the role of Lenn in the tv series *Gangs of London*, helmed by *The Raid*'s Gareth Evans. In one brutal fight, he locked horns with Elliot Finch, played by Sope Dirisu. It was a great pleasure to catch up with Lee and discuss his work to date and future aspirations, making him a very deserved entrant into the *Eastern Heroes* Hall of Fame.

SA: What was your earliest influence to become a martial Artist?
LC: I was around five years old and all my family had got together at my grandparents to watch a movie on their new VHS recorder. They had chosen two movies for us all to watch and they were *Monty Python and the Holy Grail* and *The Big Boss*. My family put *The Big Boss* on first and the movie simply changed my life. I became obsessed with Bruce Lee, I wanted to be him.

I remember when growing up, I would literally watch his movies continuously, mimicking all the moves and cries he makes (I still know the exact cries to every one of his movies haha). At Christmas all my friends were asking for BMX bikes and then there was me, kung fu suit, kung fu slippers and a pair of rubber nunchucks. As soon as I was old enough my parents enrolled me in a local karate club and, well the rest as they say was history.

SA: What movies has been the biggest influence on your career?
LC: I mean for me personally I grew up watching Bruce Lee and Jackie Chan. Growing up in the late '70s early '80s I was so lucky as literally the martial arts movie scene was incredible. There was so much to watch and get inspiration from, so much talent and so my iconic figures some of whom are now my friends, something I still shake my head about in disbelief. But if I have to pick any movies, for me *Fist of Fury, Enter the Dragon, Meals on Wheels* and *Drunken Master*… just talking about them now makes me want to watch them.

SA: How did you get involved in the film industry?
LC: This is quite an incredible story. Around 2005 I went to Los Angeles and I

the Jet has asked me to be somewhere at a certain time and that's what I'm doing ha. As it turned out the next morning I was at The Lee Strasberg and I was learning stunt performing and acting, it really was incredible.

When leaving L.A. Benny said that I was now part of his stunt team and his ambassador for the U.K., I thought that was really nice of him and a nice gesture as I was leaving. Within weeks of returning I got a call from Sensei Benny the Jet, telling me he was coming to the U.K. to make a movie and could I get some time of work and help him train the lead John Cusack. I couldn't get time off so I quit my job and off I went. It's crazy to think that one of my hero's growing up went on to be my instructor and a great friend, and be the man who gave me the opportunity to do what I do today. I will forever be in his debt for introducing me to this life.

SA: *You're in great shape and very flexible for a big guy what's your training regime?*
LC: I still train daily, obviously as I'm getting older I have to be smarter with how I train. But I have some incredible coaches that I train under, for my boxing I have pad man Steve Bates, my jujitsu/ Thai boxing Paul Sheridan, for my weight training Luke Porter from Elite and always there Master Brian McKinney.

I believe in going to bed early and getting up early and getting things done. So a normal day would see me waking up around 4am to 5am, then fit in a weights session, back refuel then midday training consisting of pads/sparring/grappling depending on days etc. And of course when I'm not away filming I teach at my martial arts Academy in the evening also. It's so important for me to do these things it has been a big part of my life since I was six years old and this will never change.

SA: *What was your experiance like working on the excellent TV series Gangs of New York and working with Gareth Edwards?*
LC: Gareth is a master at what he does; I remember getting the call asking if I would audition for the part. I was like yeah of course I will, I mean this guy revolutionised the martial arts genre and introduced a whole new level of action cinema to the world.

I watched *The Raid* with my dad and the both of us where blown away. So I jumped at the chance to audition.

When I got the role I was over the moon, I remember at rehearsals going through the fight scene and thinking to myself this is going to be pretty gnarly. It was so dark and brilliant.

First day on-set to film this scene was incredible, the set was outstanding and this completely helped with my performance.

welcomed me we hugged and chatted for a while and then he asked what I was doing whilst I was staying in LA. I said if it's alright with him I intended on spending as much time in the gym as possible but other than that I hadn't made an particular plans. He then asked Cody to write an address down on a piece of paper and handed me it and said "Be here for 9am tomorrow and bring your kit bag"

When I left the gym with my girlfriend at the time, she turned to me and said "what's the address for?" I informed her I didn't know and that all I knew was that Benny

was so desperate to train at Benny the Jet Urquidez's gym. I remember months before sending him emails stating i was making the trip and would it be possible to visit. The day I landed I got to the hotel and immediately called the gym asking would it be possible to come and visit the next day. They said of course and so the next day I jumped a cab and off I went. On arrival I was met by Cody on reception and he was so welcoming, we chatted for a bit and he asked if I wanted to go and get changed and do so training. I know this probably seems a little weird to the readers but I actually didn't take my kit with me that morning as I just wanted to go and make the right introductions first as I didn't want to be that guy, the one that turns up all cock sure and full of himself.

Cody then said I could go out back and pick some clothing from a shop at the back and he would borrow me some gloves, he didnt have to ask twice. So next thing I was in the bag area basically trying to show off and show my skills, as you do. When a lady knocked on the door, I opened it and we got speaking it was Sensei Benny's wife Sara, we chatted for a bit and then she walked away only to return and inform me she had just spoken with Benny and that he was on his way to meet me. I was completely taken back by this as Benny has been a big hero of mine for many years, not going to lie I was nervous as hell. When he got there he

Watching Gareth and Matt (his DOP) work was so masterful the understanding the both of them have with each other is perfect. The mixture of this along with working with the lead Sope Dirisu and his stunt double Mens-Sana Tamakloe just added to what was being delivered on film. Day after day we pushed on to give it everything we could, and we knew it felt special. I remember at one point when I walked out of the room with the clever Sope came up to me and said it was iconic. I'm just glad I could deliver on both my performance level with my acting as well as my performance in the fighting, the scene was incredibly well received from the viewers and I'm still now referred to as Len the Butcher. Big thanks go to Jude Poyer for his faith in me to deliver the character and also the outstanding choreography he put together with his team.

SA: You have yet to have the pleasure of working on a Hong Kong movie, is this something you would like if given the oppertunity/
LC: I would have to say that having the opportunity to work in Hong Kong would be a massive bucket list ticked for myself. Hong Kong cinema played such a massive part in my life and the amazing stars it produced where so iconic so inspirational… let's just say you wouldn't have to ask me twice. Book me that ticket ha.

SA: I recently caught up with you on The Expendables 4 *film set, how did you find the expeiraince working along side such A-List stars?*
LC: Obviously due to NDA I can't really talk about the movie at all. But having the opportunity to share the screen with Stallone was a real boyhood dream. When I message my mum and dad the pic I put "mum dad I did it, your boy did it" an incredible experience and one I'm willing to talk about more in the future when I'm allowed.

SA: The cover has had a great response with peopel suggesting this would make a great movie, what are your thoughts on this.
LC: Let's do it… it's always an honour to work Scott Adkins we've done five movies together now and have a new movie with him which is due for release next month in the USA called *One Shot* I think it's scheduled for the UK around January. Really excited for everyone to see it.

I mean Mark, Jim and Loren are all incredible and I think it would make for a

great movie… I've never worked with Jim or Loren (whom I'm a big fan) before, but Mark and myself have done a few things together and he's such a great guy.

It's funny, as I've looked up to these guys for years, and here I am now on the front cover of this incredible magazine. So thank you.

SA: What the future right now for you, as we head towards 2022, any film projects

Mark Strange

"As an actor, you want to give it 100% because once you're captured on film, you're on film forever."

that you can share with the readers?

LC: You know this year has been an incredible year for me in the film industry I've had the honour of working on some big Hollywood productions and 2022 seems to be moving in the same direction with a few projects already confirmed.

On a personal level it's about being the best dad I can be for my boy Malachi, be a good role model and continue to inspire him as much as I can. He's my motivation for everything in life, my world.

Thank you so much for having me in the magazine and the rare opportunity to grace the cover, I hope the readers have enjoyed the interview and if they want to watch my journey and see what happening then please feel free to give me a follow on media platforms. This has been an absolute pleasure and I'm really humbled…

I have had the pleasure of meeting Mark on several occasions, most recently at the UK premiere of *Ip Man 4*, for which he had travelled to Hong Kong to take part in a fight sequence with Danny Chan (who plays Bruce Lee) under the expert eye of action choreographer Yuen Woo-ping. What a fight that is! One of many highlights of the movie.

Mark, like me, is from the North. He is a much grounded man with no ego whatsoever. Yet, he has every right to be proud of his achievements! He's been fortunate enough to work alongside many amazing stars, most notably Jackie Chan in *The Medallion* and *The Twins Effect*. He also worked on *Batman Begins* and 2018's *Redcon-1*, in which he played the lead role of Lt. Frank Perez.

Once again, I considered Mark to be the perfect candidate to join the *Eastern Heroes* Hall of Fame for his significant contributions to action cinema. Ever the gentleman, he allowed me to fire some questions in his direction.

MARK WITH DANNY CHAN WHO PLAYS BRUCE LEE IN IP MAN 4

SA: *How old were you when you discovered martial arts? most people get inspiration from watching their first film.*
MS: I was ten years old when I first started practicing martial arts. My earliest interest came from watching movies! I started on Jackie Chan's work and remember enjoying those from a very young age; films like *Drunken Master* and *Snake in the Eagle's Shadow* had a big impact on me. I saw martial arts as a stepping stone to working in film.

MS: *Who was your inspiration growing up?*
MS: Jackie Chan and Jean-Claude Van Damme were always big inspirations in terms of martial arts, but my number one inspiration would be Sylvester Stallone. His career story and journey from his struggle to getting *Rocky* made, to everything he's done since, is very inspiring to me.

WITH JACKIE CHAN IN THE TWINS EFFECT

REDCON-1

SA: *You are very fit and flexible what is your typical training regime?*

MS: I mainly split between martial arts, weights and cardio. The martial arts is vital because it's my background and being an action actor, that's just what I do. I train with pads, the heavy bag and sometimes spar – plus it's crucial to stay flexible, especially with the kicking and legwork exercises. Weight training is very important to develop the physique and muscle mass needed, both in strength and also looking good on camera. Obviously you can tweak this depending on what type of role you're going for – to be bigger or smaller. I really can't emphasise how much you need to be at your physical peak for action filmmaking because it can be incredibly demanding. My focus is on keeping match fit so I am always ready for every challenge. I did a fight scene in Hong Kong on *Ip Man 4* with Danny Chan and choreographed by Yuen

Woo-ping (*The Matrix*, *Kill Bill*) and was mentally and physically tough. We were pushing ourselves to the limit to deliver the best and most memorable scene possible.

SA: *You have worked on many films, what was experience working with Jackie Chan?*

MS: He's such a cool guy and it was such a great experience working with him. He pushes you hard but at the same time he's very light hearted and really fun to be around. His energy and enthusiasm also infects the whole team so everyone really enjoys the experience.

SA: *Can you tell the readers a little bit what it was like working with director action choreographer Yuen Woo-ping on* Ip Man 4*?*

MS: I first got the call from Mike Leeder and I'm so grateful because he gave me an

opportunity and believed in my ability. It was a huge honour to be part of such a popular, iconic movie series. It was very tough, one of the most challenging jobs I've had as a performer, and I'd challenge anyone who thinks they're tough in real life to take on a Hong Kong film! What they do is on another level, and it's why those films look so good. Yuen Woo-ping is a master of his craft. He can visualise the whole scene and pieces it all together so creatively. It was an amazing experience to be part of his creative vision and to make it into reality.

I'd never worked with Master Yuen Woo-ping or Wilson Yip before, so that was a huge privilege. and worked with Donnie Yen back in 2002 on a Hong Kong film called *The Twins Effect*. Unfortunately, I wasn't on set with Donnie Yen when filing *Ip Man 4* It would have been great to see him again as I'm a big fan of his work let's see what the future holds.

SA: *You have just completed your first starring role in a new movie called* Rupture*. Can you tell us a little about your role and the movie?*

MS: *Rupture* is my first standalone lead role, due to release Summer 2022 I'm really excited for everyone to see this film, directed by Ranjeet S Marwa produced by Djonny Chen. I play the character of Raven Black in this cyber punk action thriller. Brilliant team and I'm buzzing for everyone to check out the film next year.

SA: *What does 2022 hold for you Mark?*

MS: Well I'm going to continue to grow with many cool projects in the works… got a very exciting film in development as a lead good guy. I guess everyone is just going to have to wait but I promise you it will be worth the wait to all action dans.

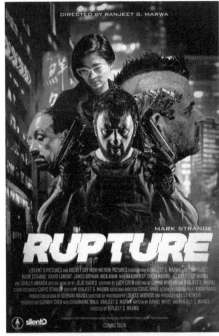

ON THE SET OF IP MAN 4

MARK WITH ACTION DIRECTOR YUEN WOO-PING

MARK WITH DIRECTOR WILSON YIP

James Bennett

"Never give up on your dream."

James is a very likeable Irish guy who crams his video chats full of good-natured banter. I consider him a good friend who always offers a fun and engaging line of conversation. Plus, he's double-hard. Need proof? Well, he started his martial arts training at the age of five, rising to a third-degree black belt in American kenpo karate. He is also well-versed in boxing, judo, Muay Thai and jiu-jitsu. That's not all – he trained in kali/eskrima (a Filipino martial art) under none other than Dan Inosanto.

Known to his friends as 'Cement Jaw', Jim put himself on the martial map by developing the story for Ireland's first martial arts film – *Fatal Deviation*. He also co-directed, co-produced and starred in it. All told, he has appeared in around twenty productions since he arrived on the scene, starring alongside Jean-Claude Van Damme, Dolph Lundgren and Mike Tyson. In recent times, he has channelled his efforts into his Los Angeles gym, encountering many celebrities in the process.

Jim's gym has rekindled his desire to get back into the film industry, and he was more than happy to talk to me about his career. I was extremely pleased that he agreed to join this issue's *Eastern Heroes* Hall of Fame, showcasing stars who are worthy of recognition and acclaim thanks to their work in Asian martial arts. I was further pleased when he agreed to be interviewed!

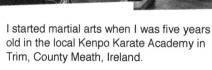
© James Bennett
(Max Havoc: Curse of the Dragon)

I started martial arts when I was five years old in the local Kenpo Karate Academy in Trim, County Meath, Ireland.

I really liked Bruce Lee and all this other action stars but my real motivation was J-CVD and *Bloodsport* and all his movies after. I loved his physique, his charisma how he kicked.

My current training regime is weight training and cardio, five days weekly, stretching every day, boxing three times weekly, Kenpo karate five days weekly, Filipino martial arts four times weekly, silat three times weekly, jkd once a week and when I'm not training I'm teaching.

My relationship with J-CVD came about when we met in the '90s. We became good friends and he would hire me to work for him. Now we hang out and train together all the time.

I think the martial arts movies today are very different compared to the '80s and '90s. They're much more aggressive today with a lot of wire work and actors portraying the characters in the '80s and '90s the martial arts you saw was more real and you had actual martial artists playing the roles.

The new cover of *Eastern Heroes* is one of the best covers I've ever seen. I believe all the action stars on the cover would make a great ensemble for and action movie! Rick Baker, Shaolin Jaa and Crike99art have done an excellent job with this cover!!

I have several projects in the pipeline as we speak one of which is a movie based in Thailand and would require an ensemble like you have on the cover of your magazine this month!!
Thank you Rick!!

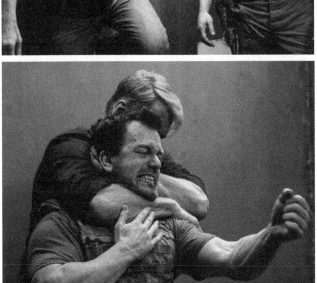

© 2015 James Bennett

straight outta Birmingham...
Scott Adkins
by Rick Baker

Out of the five people featured in this Eastern Heroes Sparta section, I have known Scott the longest. He recently spoke to me via video link from his home, which isn't a million miles away from where my mum lived in her later years. He was just off to be part of the all-star cast for *John Wick 4* that had been put together by Keanu Reeves. Sadly, I was enjoying our catch-up so much that I forgot to record our chat! I did not want to ask the questions again whilst he was shooting the epic fourth instalment of the successful franchise, so I've assembled this summary instead.

BOYKA!!

Scott is, without doubt, one of the most talented current action stars in the industry. I first met him back in the early '90s when Toby Russell and I were holding film shows at the Broadway Cinema in Nottingham. Scott was a very good looking and confident lad, whose interest in the Hong Kong martial arts movie scene was stimulated by one of my favourite films, *Tiger Cage 2*.

I remember my mum commenting that she wished Scott was her son! "What a lovely young man," she would say. "I bet his mum is proud of him!" At the time, we were doing the *Eastern Heroes Video Magazine* and had come up with the idea of getting people to shoot their own action scenes to put in a section we had called *STOP KUNG FU!*

We had some great entries. Most were just hilariously funny, but some stood out. One such clip was presented by Scott, of himself and a group of friends shooting a fight scene outside. As Toby and I viewed this, we were expecting to see yet another attempt by some young kids to try to emulate their on-screen heroes. But, no! What I watched was a very competent and well-choreographed sequence of a young Scott donning a long Crombie-style coat, and dispatching his oncoming attackers with considerable style and well-thought-out choreography.

My first words to Toby were: "He looks like a cross between Chow Yun-fat and Hugh Grant, but you know what? That kid is talented!" He even demonstrated some fancy gymnastics, performing a back flip which I rewound to check to see if he was on a wire!!

It was at that moment that a star was born. We even took that clip to present on the TV show that we were filming with Jonathan Ross, also called *STOP KUNG FU!* You can see the clip on the DVD which we gave away free in issue No. 2.

He got his first break on a movie called *Extreme Challenge* (2001), directed by Stephen Tung. You may recognise the name. He played a young student opposite Bruce Lee in *Enter the Dragon*, receiving the immortal quote:

"Don't think. FEEL. It's like a finger pointing at the moon. Do not concentrate on the finger, or you will miss all of the heavenly glory."

EXTREME CHALLENGE – *SCOTT MAKES HIS FIRST APPEARANCE*

A STAR-STUDDED CAST AT THE UK PREMIERE OF THE EXPENDABLES

Avengement

Scott did concentrate! On his career – and for that he has not missed all the heavenly glory that followed in the years to come.

Soon after working on that film, he would find himself filming alongside some of his onscreen heroes: Jackie Chan in *The Accidental Spy* (2001) and The Medallion (2003), Jet Li in *Unleashed* (aka *Danny the Dog*), and J-CVD in *The Shepherd: Border Patrol* (2008).

But it was under the watchful eye of Isaac Florentine that Scott began to flourish. Florentine had cast Adkins as 'Talbot' in *Special Forces* (2003), before elevating him to leading man status three years later. Adkins played the character 'Yuri Boyka' in *Undisputed II: Last Man Standing* in 2006, sharing top billing with Michael Jai White. When Isaac shot *Undisputed III: Redemption* in 2010, Scott once again

played the lead role, making Yuri Boyka one of the most recognisable on-screen fighters of the 21st Century.

His hard work and razor-like focus has meant that he is constantly working, in an industry that is very hard to crack. I remember talking to Scott when he attended my Hwang Jang-lee event at the O2 SENI in London back in 2014. We joked that had he been born ten years earlier, he would have been exposed to the huge VHS audience in the UK that had made stars of J-CVD, Cynthia Rothrock, Dolph Lundgren and Chuck Norris. The video market also served as a platform for Jackie Chan, as back then kung fu/martial arts-based movies went straight to video.

You do need luck to succeed in this industry, but I can say with some

confidence that Scott's rise to fame is more due to his on-screen charisma and ability to look good on screen in any fight situation.

He has also starred alongside some of Hollywood's biggest A-listers, including Sylvester Stallone, Arnold Schwarzenegger and Jason Statham. He has won three awards over the last decade or so. In 2010 he won the 'Breakout Action Star' award at the Action on Film International Festival, for his performance in *Undisputed III: Redemption*. Seven years later he claimed two awards at the Jackie Chan Action Movie Awards. For his work in the movie *Boyka: Undisputed*, he won the gongs for Best Action Movie Actor and Best Fight.

Scott has now acted, starred and fought in over sixty movies. There are simply too many to mention here! But in recent years, he has churned out some absolute gems, including a couple of my now-favourite movies. Primarily, I'm thinking of *Avengement* (2019), which I saw on the big screen at Stratford's Picturehouse with a packed audience, including Scott himself. I love prison gangster films – one of my favourite movies is *Scum* starring Ray Winstone – but after watching *Avengement* (directed by the talented Jesse V Johnson) I had to relegate *Scum* to second place. For me, it's my favourite Scott Adkins film. Another favourite is the incredibly successful *Ip Man 4*, probably dollar-for-dollar the highest-grossing kung fu movie since *Enter the Dragon*.

When I caught up with Scott via video

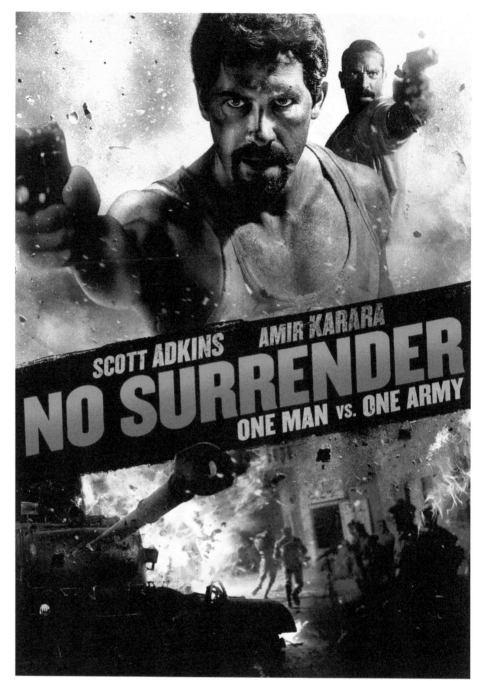

link, it was good to see that he still lives in Sutton Coldfield. He has a lovely house, which he shares with his wonderful wife Lisa, his daughter Carmel, and his son Joshua.

With Scott, you are guaranteed an excellent performance in front of the camera, but I believe that his success is also due to his grounded attitude, stable family home life and his sensible financial management. It is so easy, once you start to enjoy the trappings of fame, to be led away from your path. But not Scott. He is living his best life and it is richly deserved.

During my chat with Scott, he was about to fly out to join Keanu Reeves on the set of the fourth instalment of the *John Wick* franchise, which also meant that he was due to be reunited with his *Ip Man 4*

co-star Donnie Yen. We could not talk too much about it at that time, but Scott was excited to tell me about his latest project. *One Shot* is an action movie that is filmed in real time, in one continuous shot.

Now, as we go to print, *One Shot* has just been released on 5th November. Sadly, I could not get to see it before sending this issue off, but I did get to see the trailer a

SCOTT AND DIRECTOR JAMES NUNN

few weeks ago, which had just dropped whilst I was on the set of *The Expendables 4*. Lee A Charles, who was working on the movie, walked up and gave me my first preview. Lee is also in *One Shot*, so he too was excited to see this.

It looks like Scott has once again raised his game, to deliver an exciting new concept to his ever-growing fan base. He told me that he is very proud of this film, and he was excited to be once again working alongside director James Nunn. Nunn has worked with Scott on several previous movies, enabling them to establish a good relationship with genuine chemistry, the fruits of which I believe you can see on-screen. I am excited to see this, and know it will be 'up there' in the Scott Adkins Stellar Performances Archive.

I have watched from afar as Scott's career has gone from strength to strength, and I feel so proud of him. The local boy has done well! I like to think that I played a very tiny part in his career development, if only via turning him onto Hong Kong movies, and featuring his home-made video both in *Eastern Heroes Video Magazine* and my TV show *STOP KUNG FU!* (2001).

Thank you, Scott, for your time, and I know that 2022 and beyond will see your career continue to grow. I will be watching and cheering as I have done for the past thirty years!

SCOTT WITH DONNIE YEN ON SET – IP MAN 4

DIRECTOR JESSIE V JOHNSON AND SCOTT ADKINS ON THE SET OF AVENGEMENT

SCOTT AND THE LEGENDARY YUEN WOO-PING

AL LEONG'S HOLLYWOOD Stories

by Al Leong,
with Jason McNeil

A Quick Non-Introduction from Jas: It always bugs me when someone says a star 'needs no introduction' then immediately starts a lengthy introduction, but in this case, its absolutely true. If you're reading *Eastern Heroes*, you know who Al Leong is. The guy's got 123 film and movie credits and is the perennial kung fu badass henchman by which all other kung fu badass henchmen are measured. If you've ever been fortunate enough to talk with Al, you'll discover he's a sweetheart and a genuinely good guy who also NEVER hesitates to tell you what he really thinks. With that in mind, let's pull up a chair and settle in for an exclusive trip behind the scenes of some of your favorite movies, courtesy of Uncle Al.

BIG TROUBLE IN LITTLE CHINA

It seemed like every Asian in the motion picture industry was working on the set of *Big Trouble in Little China*… except me. The stunt coordinator, Kenny Endoso, didn't know me – therefore, I was not going to work on the movie. Then [director] John Carpenter spotted me and asked if I was working on his film. I said that I was not, and he put me on, himself!

John Carpenter is an incredible man. In the movie business, everybody thinks they're God, but John is the type of person that anybody can walk up and talk to. His wife, Sandy King is also a great person, and produced all of John's movies after *Big Trouble*. They have a beautiful home high in the hills above the Sunset Strip, which I have been invited to many times. Thanks, John, for putting me in your movie!

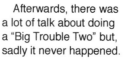

Afterwards, there was a lot of talk about doing a "Big Trouble Two" but, sadly it never happened.

ALL PHOTOS COURTESY OF AL LEONG

THE TWILIGHT ZONE
Another TV show that I enjoyed doing was *The Twilight Zone*. (NO! Not the original black and white series with Rod Serling! That was 1959! I'm not that old! Heh heh…) It was in glorious color and starring Elliot Gould.

The episode was called *Mrs Fortune Cookie* and, unfortunately (see what I did, there?) I have only seen it once, when it originally aired. For some reason, they never seem to air it when they have those '*Twilight Zone* Marathons'. Ah, well…

LETHAL WEAPON
Lethal Weapon was another fun film to work on. Mel Gibson, Danny Glover and Gary Busey were terrific to work with, along with stunt coordinator, Bobby Bass, whom we called the 'Bass Master'! Richard Donner did an excellent job directing the movie, which grossed more than $65 million at the box office, and set the stage for three sequels!

RAPID FIRE
Now here's a strange story: Before the movie began, they called me in to read for a part with a lot of dialogue. I went in and TOTALLY screwed it up! But

FUN SIDEBAR:
File this one under 'Should have done it'. A guy approached me and said he had seen me in *Lethal Weapon* and had an idea for a MOVIE SERIES with me as the star! He said he had written three scripts, with me in mind as the lead, who was a bad guy in all three films, then, at the very end it was revealed that I was not the bad guy at all, but actually a good guy! The idea sounded good, but he had no buyers at the time, so I had to pass...

what's funny is, a week later, they called me back to read more dialogue for the same character! I went in again and totally screwed it up AGAIN! Then, about two weeks later, they called me back again. And, again, I totally screwed it up!

Why? Well, number one, I am not an actor and number two, I never really expected to be called back after the first time, much less the second. I think they originally considered me for the character that ended up being played by Tzi Ma (who, by the way, did an excellent job!)

I ended up as a different character, who went up against Brandon Lee in the final fight! It was a fight that would usually have taken three nights to a week to film, but we were pressed for time and we did it in one evening! Dwight Little did an unbelievable job filming it, Brandon Lee was incredible to work with and Jeff Imada, whom I have

worked with quite often, did a great job as stunt coordinator, along with the crew!

Unfortunately, I didn't get paid for it! Because I had come over to shoot the scene in the middle of working on another movie in Hawaii, the producer (who I call a Nobody Producer who somehow got the job and wanted to make things rough for me) said that, since I was already working in Hawaii, he wasn't required to pay me, because one cannot work two jobs at the same time. I think we fought over this for at least three months. Then he called the Screen Actors Guild, because he feared I'd chase him down and put him in his place! Disappointingly, the Screen Actors Guild backed him up.

TWILIGHT ZONE AGAIN!

I also worked on the feature film version of *The Twilight Zone* but I was not there for the infamous day that everyone talks about.

The scene I was in was being shot out in Indian Dunes, which is a motocross park, and I had actually broken my leg the day before, riding a dirt bike there. They weren't happy, because I didn't call and tell them I had broken my leg, but they ended up covering the leg so it looked like it was a wartime accident. I think I worked for three days.

On the last day, I spoke with Vic Morrow. The next day, he was killed on set in a tragic helicopter accident.

COBRA (ALMOST)

On Sylvester Stallone's movie, *Cobra*, I was chosen to play one of the leads! Those of you who have seen the movie, though, will not recall having seen me in that role. Here's how that silliness happened:

I read for the part in casting, and they told me that I got the part! But later, some Asian group protested because they hated the idea of an Asian bad guy, so I was removed from the movie!

Sly Stallone is one person I wish I could have fought on the big screen. I hate these stupid protest groups who have no idea what is going on!

DIE HARD

This was, without a doubt, a fun film to work on. Charlie Picerni did a fantastic job as stunt coordinator and all the terrorists were great to hang around, as was Reginald VelJohnson, who played the cop who communicated with Bruce Willis from outside the building. After the shoot, I continued to hang out with Dennis Hayden.

It was during this time that I was called to fight Sylvester Stallone on another movie, but *Die Hard* wouldn't release me because they didn't know when they might need me! (All the actors were on hold for so long because the script was being rewritten.)

People tend to reminisce about my character 'Uli' the terrorist with a sweet

AL HASSLES THE HOFF! (ON THE SET OF KNIGHT RIDER.)

LITTLE KNOWN FACT! AL LEONG KILLED GODZILLA AND HAD THE HEAD MOUNTED AS A TROPHY!!! (NOT TRUE! HOWEVER, IT SHOULD BE NOTED THAT SINCE 1963, WHEN AL MOVED TO LOS ANGELES, GODZILLA HAS ATTACKED TOKYO, NEW YORK CITY, LAS VEGAS AND SAN FRANCISCO, BUT NEVER ONCE SET FOOT IN HOLLYWOOD!)

BARELY TWO YEARS AFTER TORTURING MEL GIBSON IN LETHAL WEAPON AL LEONG "TOTALLY RAVAGED OSHMAN'S SPORTING GOODS" AS GENGHIS KHAN IN BILL AND TED'S EXCELLENT ADVENTURE (1989)!

tooth. If I remember correctly, the candy bars I stole and ate were a Mars Bar and a Nestle's Crunch.

GHOSTS OF MARS

On another John Carpenter film, *Ghosts of Mars*, I had a big fight scene with Ice Cube. However, none of that footage ended up on the screen. Here again, maybe it was decided that the scene would've distracted from the actual movie, so none of the footage was used.

BILL AND TED'S EXCELLENT ADVENTURE

Bill and Ted was another fun film to work on, where I got to actually use my Kwan dao skills onscreen as Genghis Khan! Keanu Reeves and Alex Winter were MOST EXCELLENT to work with, along with director Stephen Herek, stunt coordinator Dan Bradley (also excellent!) and all the sidekicks who worked with me! Also, it was in Arizona, which is always a most excellent place to shoot!

DOUBLE DRAGON

On *Double Dragon* Jeff Imada brought a lot of stunt guys from Los Angeles to Cincinnati, Ohio, to work, and I had a terrific time doing a fight with Mark Dacascos, who is a great martial artist in his own right! (I remember first meeting Mark when he was very young, and I was competing against his parents in martial arts tournaments back then!)

Jeff and I played the two sidekicks for Robert Patrick (the bad guy, of course) and we were actually allowed to create the whole ending as we walked away ad-libbing dialogue!

LETHAL WEAPON 4

On *Lethal Weapon 4* I did an extensive fight scene with Danny Glover. I believe we spent four days on the fight – however, the footage was not released! As I understand it, the producers felt that, since I was killed in *Lethal Weapon 1*, me briefly appearing in Part 4 would not work.

THE REPLACEMENT KILLERS

On the set of *Replacement Killers*, a Chow Yun-fat action movie, we were in an alleyway in downtown Los Angeles, where it was very dirty. We were filming the finale scene, so the alley was pretty packed with cast and crew. The stunt coordinator, Allan Graf, was standing in the middle of the alley, carrying a huge stick over his shoulder to try to beat the huge rats that were also in the alley – and there were plenty of them! I was along the edge of the alley about twenty feet away and, since I was in the scene, I had a clear shot at him. My right foot was along the wall and a huge rat was walking right towards me! When the rat moved to my foot and was halfway on top, I kicked the rat up – and I knew EXACTLY where it was going! A lot of the people just backed away when they saw the rat in the air, but Allan didn't, so it IT HIT HIM SQUARE IN THE CHEST!

(Perhaps understandably) the whole 'flying rat in the chest thing' got him extremely upset, and he told me there would be no 'stunt adjustment' bonus in my paycheck for that day!

VENGEANCE UNLIMITED

Michael Madsen is a fantastic man who had a TV show for one season called *Vengeance Unlimited*. I was a stunt coordinator on the show which, unfortunately, went up against *Friends* in its time slot, so we had problems trying to get an audience. Which is sad, because it was a really awesome show – excellently written, brilliantly acted and the crew behind the camera was fantastic! They really knew what they were doing! It was a show that easily could've run for five seasons but, because of the placement, it didn't have a chance.

(**Jas Note:** *I had never heard of this show until Al told me about it – which is weird, because I'm a huge Michael Madsen fan, and even moved heaven and earth to have him as a guest on my TV show,* Stars-Stunts-Action! *If you can chase down the DVD box set, do yourself a favour and watch it! Imagine the premise of* The Equalizer *but starring Mr. Blonde! It is eighteen kinds of awesome! And, of course, I mean the original* Equalizer, *not the current one where Queen Latifah is supposed to be writing wrongs and fighting the forces of evil, but instead spends most of every episode arguing with her teenage daughter. But, I digress. Time for one more BTS story from Al!*)

No, they didn't get him to shave his head! Perish the thought! It's a bald wig.

Jas and Al with Jeff Imada (left) at a Whiskey Bar in Little Tokyo. (No, I'm not going to give you the backstory. Use your imagination.)

THE SCORPION KING

Stunt Coordinator Billy Burton, with whom I had previously worked on a TV series called *Simon & Simon*, brought me on as the fight choreographer for a film called The *Scorpion King*, starring Dwayne Johnson, who is known in the wrestling world as 'The Rock'. Kelly Hu played the leading lady – she is fantastic and someone I've been fortunate enough to work with many times. Steven Brand did an incredible job, along with Michael Clarke Duncan, whom I had briefly met a few years earlier when I covered for Jeff Imada on *The Green Mile*. Michael was nominated but he did not win an Academy Award for that role.

'The Rock' was on an extremely tight schedule on that shoot. He was driven to the training hall at a certain time and was set to leave at a certain time with a limo waiting! Nevertheless, he was totally relaxed and calm and completely what I call 'in tune'. I don't think anyone can say that they actually taught 'The Rock' because he just walks in the door and is ready to go! We're talking about long choreographed fights, over a table, spinning and rolling, up a long set of steps, around obstacles, against double swords which were really on fire (not computer generated!) In fact, he was so in tune, I wish they would've left more full-figure (wide) shots of him in action against the swordsman!

We had about a dozen good-sized fights, at least four of which never made it on screen because of script and location changes!

The choice of weapons constantly changed. I worked with the actors using a variety of weapons so they could be prepared for the final decision. Some of the choreographed sequences I worked out were totally scrapped because of the weapon changes. I originally had 'The Rock' with a huge bladed weapon, but later Chuck Russell, the director, decided that Dwayne with this huge blade just looked too overpowering!

The original fight had Steven Brand fighting with only one sword. After about a week with Steven, Chuck asked me how he was progressing. I said he was doing great. Chuck said "Good, put another sword in his other hand!" In later meetings, it was decided to put the swords on fire as

well! Personally, I think they just thought it would be nice to have a barbecue on set!

Before the film was released, I was called to do a short fight scene with Tony McEwing, a newscaster on Channel 11. The location was in front of a *Scorpion King* billboard about thirty feet in the air above Sunset Boulevard and Crescent Heights! So we climbed up, I set up a short sword fight between Tony and me and, even though I was told he wasn't feeling very well, he did a great job and we pulled it off! News at 11!!!

About the authors:

Al Leong is a living legend. A champion martial artist, fan favorite character actor, A-list stunt coordinator, fight coordinator and stuntman, motorcycle enthusiast, Chinese lion dance record holder, stuffed animal collector, author and dad. If you liked this article and want more, check out his excellent autobiography, *The Eight Lives of Al 'Ka-Bong' Leong* and the 2018 documentary *Henchman: The Al Leong Story*.

Jason McNeil – "Put this in: Al says Jason knows his stuff and is the best at what he does." — Al Leong

Al Leong does some high kicking

Spotlight on
The King of the
SOUTHERN FIST

王道

Don Wong Tao – Wang Tao, Wong Tou, Wang Dao, Don Wang Tao. Born: 1950 (Taiwan)

Wang Tao, sometime referred to as Don Wang Tao, has been a favorite of kung fu film fans for many years, especially those who looked outside of Shaw Brothers and Golden Harvest for premium kung fu action.

With his good looks and heroic roles, Wang Tao cemented himself in the annals of kung fu movie history as a bankable star. Wang Tao started on a very different path. Born in South Korea of Chinese ancestry, he earned his black belt in the kicking-oriented martial art of Tae Kwon Do. While studying at the University of Texas, he was approached by Golden Harvest execs to be in an upcoming film. While he made an appearance in *Chinatown Capers* (aka *Back Alley Princess*), Wang would debut and star opposite *Way of the Dragon* antagonist and multi-time American tournament champion Chuck Norris.

THE
SECRET
RIVALS

This film is *Slaughter in San Francisco*, or *Yellow-Faced Tiger*. Although not a commercial success, it wet Wang's appetite for more kung fu movie action.

When Seasonal Films and Ng See-yuen came calling for the film *Secret Rivals*, Wang answered. He starred opposite two other leg-fighting superstars, John Liu and Hwang Jang-lee (arguably the best kicker in kung fu cinema). Wang was to play the hero again in the role of Sheng Ying-wei, a southern fist expert, to match up with the northern legs styles of Shao Yi-fei (John Liu) and Silver Fox (Hwang Jang-lee). This casting choice made a difference in the persona Wang would take on in many of his subsequent films. The problem was that Wang was a Tae Kwon Do man and really didn't have the dexterity in his hand techniques to pull of the southern fist style the script called for. Cue in frequent collaborator and fight choreographer Gam Ming (Tommy Lee). According to an audio interview with Wang Tao himself, Gam Ming worked with him extensively to polish his hand techniques. The result was the on-screen fighting Wang Tao was known for throughout the rest of his kung fu career that gave him the nickname, 'King of the Southern Fist'. Under Gam Ming's instruction, Wang became quite adept at southern kung fu hand motions.

Wang Tao is one of the few non-Shaw or Non-Golden Harvest kung fu stars that developed a cult-like following in the United States due to his appearance in *The Hot, Cool and The Vicious*. He co-starred with fellow Tae Kwon Do expert 'Flash Legs' Tan Tao-liang, and Gam Ming, his real-life father George Wang Chueh under the expert direction of Taiwan's Lee Tso-nam. Again, he portrayed a master of fist techniques while 'Flash Legs' handled the kicking action and Gam Ming mixing potent kicking techniques with mantis-style hand motions. The result was a cult

classic that has been referenced in hip-hop songs and other areas of American pop culture.

Wang Tao had some interesting pairings with other kung fu stars in some of his films. We have already mentioned 'northern leg' experts 'Flash Legs' Tan Tao-liang and John Liu (by the way he was a student of Tan Tao-liang) but one of Wang's most memorable team-up films was *Shaolin Iron Claws*. In that movie, he played the righteous Commander Hu and was paired up with Li I Min. Li was a student of Peking Opera in Taiwan. This time, Li I Min was the double-crossing Ping Long who must ultimately fight with Commander Hu (Wang Tao) to defeat the evil Manchurian Court representative (Chang Yi). LI I Min also starred in such Chang Cheh classics as *Shaolin Temple*, *The Brave Archer* and *Heaven and Hell*, and had lead roles in non-Shaw kung fu classics including as *The Mystery of Chess Boxing*, *7 Commandments of Kung Fu* and *The 7 Grandmasters*.

THE HOT,
THE COOL AND
THE VICIOUS

THE HOT THE COOL AND VICIOUS

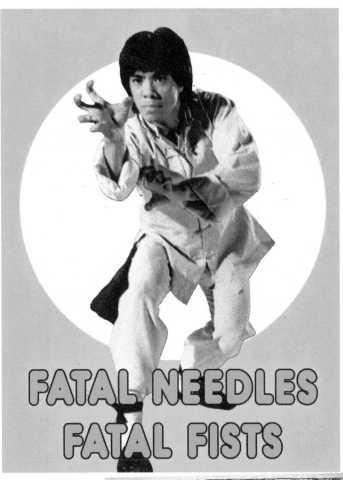

FATAL NEEDLES FATAL FISTS

DISCIPLE OF SHAOLIN MASTER

Starring WONG TAO . LO CHI YEH . LUNG FEI . CHEN HUI LAU . JACKY LEE
Produced by CHEUNG KAM FONG . Action Director CHAN LUNG YI
Directed by EUGENE HSIEH

In these movies, Wang Tao hit his stride with his 'King of the Southern Fist' persona was in full swing. Without a doubt, one of my favorite Lee Tso-nam directed films starring Wang Tao is *Fatal needles vs. Fatal Fists*. This time, instead of having a great partner to team up with Wang gets a great adversary to play off of: Chung Tung, the Mongolian Bandit. Chung, played by screen vet Chang Yi is the perfect villain for our hero Chen Chieh to fight. While Chen (Wang Tao) is righteous and law abiding, Chung is a ruthless drug smuggler whose name strikes fear into the hearts of ordinary kung fu men! The twists and turns of the plot are worth the final fight between these two as we learn brain wins over brawn every time.

Not content to just to stay in front of the

camera, Wang Tao directed and starred in *Along Came a Tiger*. This film has the tone of a western with kung fu elements and Wang does his best to bring out the uniqueness of Miracle Man. The cast includes Phillip Kao Fei, Doris Lung Chung Er, Wu Ma and Gam Ming (all recognizable and big names in Taiwanese kung fu cinema).

In addition to Ching Dynasty and other historic settings in kung fu movies, Wang has starred in

contemporary cops and robbers action films such as *Wild Panther*, *Thunder Cops*, and *Final Judgement*. Wang Tao's realistic-looking fighting style (and of course the choreography of Gam Ming and Peng Kang) helped him make the transition from period pieces to the contemporary action thrillers.

Here at Film Fan Dojo, Taiwanese kung fu cinema (and Taiwanese Wu Xia cinema) is an interesting topic and one which we will explore more in depth. Wang Tao is an undeniable part of the great heritage of Taiwanese kung fu and action movies. His persona as 'The King of the Southern Fist' is an indispensable part of our kung

fu movie viewing and Wang holds a special place among the top tier of martial arts stars, at least in our humble opinion. Wang Tao is truly 'The King of the Southern Fist'.

WANG TAO

王道 **Filmography**

Chinatown Capers (1974) … *Yellow-Faced Tiger*
Yellow Faced Tiger (1974) … *Don Wong [intro]*
The Secret Rivals (1976) … *Sheng Ying-wei*
The Hot, the Cool and the Vicious (1976) … *Pai Yu-ching*
Revenge of Kung Fu Mao (1977) … *Kang*
Endless Fight (1977) … *[Guest]*
The Proud Horses in Flying Sand (1977) … *Kokochin (Ko Ko Chen)*
18 Swirling Riders (1977) … *Hu Yu-han*
Duel with Death (1977) … *Hero*
Along Comes a Tiger (1977)
Two Assassins of the Darkness (1977) … *Dagger Kuan*
Ten Brothers of Shaolin (1977) … *One of the Ten Brothers*
The Fight for Shaolin Tamo Mystique (1977) … *Chang Shan Feng*
Eagle's Claw (1977) … *Li Chi*
Moonlight Sword and Jade Lion (1977)
Warlock of the Battlefield (1977) … *Captain Yang Chuan-Chung*
The Damned (1977) … *Shang Li*
Snaky Knight Fight Against Mantis (1978) … *Ah Fu*
Iron Swallow (1978) … *Tu Lung*
Assault of Final Rival (1978) … *Chen Wai, Shaggy Dog*
Shaolin Iron Claws (1978) … *Commander Hou*
Phantom Kung Fu (1978) … *Shao Yu Pai*
Tiger Man (1978) … *Don Won*
Kung Fu of Dammoh Styles (1978) … *Secret Agent*
Challenge of Death (1978) … *Chen Sao-wan*
Fatal Needles Vs. Fatal Fists (1978) … *Meng Hu/Chin Chai*
Right Overcomes Might (1978)
Shaolin Invincible Sticks (1978) … *Chen Ku Yung*
Shaolin Kung Fu Master (1978) … *Wan Lung*
Adventure for Imperial Treasure (1979) … *Hsiao Ching*
Eunuch of the Western Palace (1979)
Death Duel of Kung Fu (1979) … *Sun Shing-kwei*
Quick Step Mantis (1979)
The Battle of Guningtou (1979) … *Fisherman*
The Pioneers (1980)
Island Warriors (1981) … *Lu [uncredited]*
Diamond Fight (1981)
The Battle for the Republic of China (1981) … **Peng Chu-fan**
Bird's Fly (1982)
I Shall Return (1982)
The Anger (1982)
Night Orchid (1982)
The Battle of Erdan (1982)
The Girl Robber and I (1982)
Devil Returns (1982) … *Tu*
Blood Brothers (1982)
Happy Days in the Army (1982)
Strange Skill (1982)
Impossible Woman (1982) … *Chief Fu*
Crisis (1983) … *Boss Ying Tzu*
Kidnapped (1983) … *Jow Shih-jen*
The Night Ever So Long (1983)
Ninja Thunderbolt (1984) … *[To Catch a Thief footage]*
The Story in Sorghum Field (1984)
Inferno Thunderbolt (1984) … *[Footage from The Anger]*
The Express (1984)
Wild Panther (1984)

To Catch a Thief (1984) … *Inspector Wang Lei*
Man Niu De Er Zi (1984)
Drunken Tai Chi (1984) … *Ta Sha's father*
Women Warriors of Kinmen (1985) … *Wang Yi*
Wu Nu (1985)
The Kinmen Bombs (1986)
The Story of Dr. Sun Yat Sen (1986)
Promising Young Boy (1987) … *Tiger Mon*
Be My Lovely Child Again (1987)
When the Ocean Is Blue (1988)
Angel of Vengeance (1993)
Magic Sword (1993)
Hi Sir (1996)
Temptress of a Thousand Face (1998) … *Chung Yuan-kuei*
Final Judgement (1999)
Thunder Cops (1999)
Hector (2000)
Born to Be King (2000) … *Dragon*
A Matter of Time (2000)
The Love Winner (2004) … *Dao lam*
Wolf (2005) … *Howard's gang boss*
Ballistic (2008)
Will You Still Love Me (2011)
My Mandala (2012) … *Hu Ting-han*
First of May (2015)
Yes, Sir 7 (2016)
The Gap (2016) … *Father Li*

KING of the KICKERS 黃正利

An interview with HWANG JANG LEE

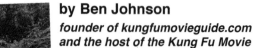

In a film career spanning over two decades as the archetypal go-to martial arts movie villain, Hwang Jang Lee kicked out Jackie Chan's teeth and wore some of kung fu cinema's most elaborate wigs. Then he disappeared. So what happened? I meet up with the world's original bootmaster to find out.

by Ben Johnson
founder of kungfumovieguide.com and the host of the Kung Fu Movie Guide Podcast. Interview originally published in October 2014 with revisions made by the author.

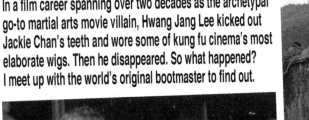

If there was ever a performer who best encapsulated maniacal villainy during the golden age of kung fu cinema, then it was the inimitable Hwang Jang Lee. In his debut Hong Kong feature, *The Secret Rivals* (1976), he set the template, playing the wizened Ming dynasty bandit, Silver Fox, complete with furrowed brow, long white locks and matching beard. He embodied bloated aristocrats, oppressive warlords, corrupt officials and tyrants who persecuted the weak and exploited the poor – perpetually cast (or, rather, typecast) as hard bastards who spent their time accumulating wealth and power, either to protect their own position or their bodies from physical attack. As the devious guard in *Invincible Armour* (1977), not even swords can harm him. As the cunning Eagle Claw fighter in *Snake in*

the Eagle's Shadow (1978), he manipulates the film's young and impressionable hero – played by Jackie Chan – into revealing the whereabouts of his own master.

Being of Korean descent, he was the ubiquitous outsider of Hong Kong cinema who moved with an alien poise and intensity. At his disposal, a legacy of trademark kicks. John Liu and Dorian Tan may lay claim to the word, but for me, the term 'bootmaster' belongs to Hwang Jang Lee. His physical dexterity, honed from a background in Taekwondo, meant he was capable of unique, gravity-defying kicks, regularly slowed down on film to savour the agility of his movements and the satisfying moment of impact. Directors used Hwang's kicks in an almost fetishist display of pugilism – and his influence on kung fu movies was vast. When Jackie Chan returned to his most famous kung fu film for its sequel, *Drunken Master II* (1994), he employed Ken Lo to play a high-kicking villain in tribute to the franchise's original baddie – the deadly 'Thunderfoot', played, inevitably, by Hwang Jang Lee.

In over sixty film appearances, he went toe-to-toe with the likes of Sammo Hung, Cynthia Rothrock, Moon Lee and Michelle Yeoh. Then, in 1996 – after over

two decades in the film industry – he disappeared. Rumours abound as to where and, crucially, what he had been doing in the years that followed. In the 1990s, sudden exits from the Hong Kong film industry were not uncommon. Many actors – Brigitte Lin, Cherie Chung, and even Michelle Yeoh – went from huge stars to disappearing acts. It was widely reported that Hwang Jang Lee had moved back to his native Seoul. Then there were rumours as to the specifics of his new business ventures, each more curious than the next. One claimed he had opened a hotel. There was talk of him running an agency for bodyguards. The most abstract career move I remember reading was on the liner notes of an Eastern Heroes VHS tape, which said Hwang Jang Lee had turned his back on the film industry to open a factory manufacturing golf tees.

So it was with a sense of incredulity that I heard the news that not only was the reclusive Hwang still very much among us, but that he would be travelling to the UK to hold a seminar at the annual SENI martial arts expo in 2014. A week later and I am sat across from him in the plush surrounds of a London hotel. Aged 69, he sports calloused knuckles and appears to be in incredible shape. You would think he was middle aged rather than a man approaching his dotage. He is smaller than he appears in his films, and laughs incessantly between answering in broken English (throughout our interview he is joined by an interpreter). It's not quite the picture I was expecting from his snarling film persona. He is open, engaged, and given this is his first visit to the UK, clearly flattered by his appeal in the west. Then it suddenly dawns on me: where the hell has he been for the last twenty years, and why has he left it so late to tell his story?

"Because he had been living in Hong Kong for quite a long time, it was too much," he says via a translator. "He wanted to go back to Korea. In the beginning, he did make more films, but he also owned a lot of business industries." Ah, the golf tee story! So was that true? "Yeah, yeah, I stayed and make the golf tee," he says smiling. "I followed a company in America, and they buy my golf tee, and I had that business for a long, long time." Did you make any money? "Hmm… not so much!" He laughs again. So what about the hotel? "Hotel – yeah! First time it was a good business, but afterwards, not so good [because] I'm not there! Someone else took care of it. That was the problem." Given how candidly he speaks, I figure I might as well ask him about the bodyguard agency. "That was for a short time," he says. "I think, 'it's not so good', so it closed."

Of course, Hwang hasn't been completely absent from our screens. In recent years, he has been enjoying something of a renaissance. In 2009, he

Chinese?!' 'No, I'm Korean!' They seem surprised. Because when I was young, I spent a lot of time in Hong Kong, I think over twenty years I lived there, so [to them] I'm just… Chinese." This notion of displacement has been a common theme throughout Hwang Jang Lee's multifaceted life. He was born in Japan in 1944, where his father worked in the shipping industry. His family were forced to return to their native Korea following Japan's defeat in the Second World War. He first started training in Taekwondo at the age of fourteen and soon progressed to 7th dan black belt. In the early 1960s, Hwang was conscripted into the Korean army where he spent years teaching martial arts to the troops for use in real-life combat situations. He taught in the famed Tiger Division of the Korean army, which supported the South Vietnamese during the Vietnam War. Later, on film sets, Hwang would obtain a certain notoriety for not holding back during his fight scenes. He famously (and accidentally) kicked out one of Jackie Chan's teeth during the filming of the climactic fight scene in *Snake in the Eagle's Shadow*.

"All actors pretended to do martial arts. But I am a real martial arts actor. I didn't pretend to do it," he says. "These days, many young actors search on the internet for the martial arts and they borrow the martial arts – it's not real. When they make a film, sometimes when there is a demonstration, they use a rope for effect, but [the audience] notice very quickly if it is real or it is fake. While I'm making a film, doing martial arts with wires [caused me] a problem, because I cannot control myself. It's not convenient. It's not real."

Hwang was well-placed to capitalise on the 1970s kung fu movie boom, and to supplement his career as an instructor, he started appearing in a number of small-budget Korean fight films. He was soon discovered by the highly influential Hong Kong producer Ng See-yuen, who was filming in Korea after leaving Shaw Brothers to start his own company, Seasonal Films. Hwang Jang Lee's first film for Seasonal, *The Secret Rivals* (1976), highlighted his superb kicking abilities, and he became an overnight success in Hong Kong. Ng had to personally fight to keep Hwang in the country after being questioned about his work credentials. Ng, in conversation with Bey Logan in his book Hong Kong Action Cinema, described how immigration officials questioned him as to why he couldn't use a local actor for the role, to which he replied: "You get me someone local who can kick like him and I will."

Ng would continue to cast him as the villain in many of his best films over the next decade, including more John Liu helmers, like *Snuff Bottle Connection* (1977) and *Invincible Armour*, the Jackie Chan films *Snake in the Eagle's Shadow* and *Drunken*

appeared in a Korean TV series called *The Return of Iljimae*. It marked his first screen appearance in thirteen years. The move sparked a reappraisal of his career among kung fu movie fans, particularly in the west, which prompted the American filmmaker Jon-James Hodson to make his 2013 documentary, *The Anonymous King*. This

60-minute film sees Hodson unravel the myths surrounding Hwang's disappearance from the film industry and tracks him down to his home in Seoul to discuss his life and career.

"In Korea, they think I'm Chinese, not Korean," he laughs. "Even now, too! It's very strange, you know. 'You're not

Master (1978), the official *Drunken Master* sequel, *Dance of the Drunk Mantis* (1979), the bizarre Bruceploitation flick, *Game of Death II* (1981), and Hwang's only English-language film, *No Retreat, No Surrender 2: Raging Thunder* (1988), opposite Cynthia Rothrock. Does he have a favourite?

"*Drunken Master*," he says, without hesitation. "It was really interesting. I was proud of myself [in the film]." It's a bona fide classic, and well deserving of its place in the kung fu movie hall of fame, but did he realise he was making a masterpiece? "I believed it would be widespread," he says. "In the company [Seasonal Films], he [Jackie Chan] was already signed and they had to make a film together. I had never heard of him. *Drunken Master* and *Snake in the Eagle's Shadow* – that's when I knew Jackie Chan and Yuen Woo-ping. Yuen Woo-ping tried very hard to think about how to control the fight. He was always thinking. Yeah, [he is] one of the best."

His performances in both *Snake* and *Drunken Master* were career-defining and opened the door to many similar roles.

THE USUAL SUSPECTS FAN IT UP WITH HWANG

Was he not concerned about always playing the villain? "I wanted to be the bad guy," he says. "In the film, the bad guy can dress up [and look] very rare and good-looking. The good person in the film, they dress like a beggar – a poor person."

Tellingly, however, when the opportunity came to produce and direct his own film – the brilliant *Hitman in the Hand of Buddha* (1981) – he removed the silver wigs, shaved off the beard, and cast himself as the hero. He even expanded into slapstick routines as a kung fu pauper opposite a sifu beggar, played by Fan Mei-sheng. "I was always acting, so I understood film, and the feeling, so it was easy as a director. But I had to take responsibility for the film, because the director's name is my name – and I am from Korea!"

Although Hwang adjusted naturally to the quick pace of Hong Kong fight choreography, he says he took time to adjust to the food, language and culture of his new home. Even without knowing any Cantonese or English, he continued to teach martial arts when living in Hong Kong. One of his students was the American fighter and actor Roy Horan, who first met Hwang on the set of *Bruce Lee's Secret* (1976). Hwang lived with Horan in Taipei when he first moved to China, and Horan would go on to produce an instructional film to help promote his sifu's amazing abilities. *The Art of High Impact Kicking* (1981) is a strange pseudo-documentary which mixes choreographed fight sequences with scenes of Hwang performing straight-to-camera drills in a dojo setting. The variety and creativity in his kicks is extraordinary. He says they were all his idea. "The jumping three kicks, spinning kicks, the flying kicks, that's all me. It's really difficult. Nobody can do it, apart from me." So how did he know he could do it in the first place? "I think, 'if I try one more step, just one more step, then I can do it'. So I did."

I ask him about the Horan documentary, but he can't remember making it. I'm not surprised. It was made during a particularly prolific phase in his career which Roy Horan believes was the

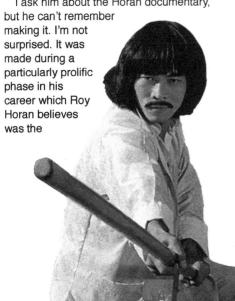

making of his undoing. Horan told *HKCinemagic* in 2006 that Hwang's box office had suffered after appearing in so many films, and "some quite poor ones". Hwang's work in the 1980s became increasingly sporadic, despite supporting roles in some huge Hong Kong hits, including Sammo Hung's all-star 1986 eastern-western, *Millionaire's Express* (where he was cast as a Japanese Samurai), and the Michelle Yeoh adventure, *Magnificent Warriors* (1987). He went

into TV work, before eventually leaving Hong Kong to return to South Korea. Despite his high impact on screen, Hwang quietly retired in 1996.

Despite the transient nature of fame and fortune, it is Hwang's dedication to the martial arts which has remained a consistent force in his life. At SENI, he holds a seminar in front of more than 50 eager paying customers, and he can still spin and kick in much the same way he always could. He is a technical advisor for the World Tang Soo Do General Federation – an historic Korean fighting art which predates Taekwondo. Cynthia Rothrock and Chuck Norris are also practitioners. He still trains, but now, it's all about training the mind. "There is one standard, and if you are over this standard, you can just train your mind and you can do anything," he says. "This is what I call Hwang Jang Lee Martial Arts. It is my principle."

Follow Hwang Jang Lee on Facebook and Instagram. Thank you to Toby Russell and Ricky Baker at Eastern Heroes for arranging this interview. Original article published on kungfumovieguide.com in October 2014, with revisions made by the author. Ben Johnson is the founder of kungfumovieguide.com and the host of the Kung Fu Movie Guide Podcast, featuring interviews with the biggest names in martial arts movies, available everywhere you get podcasts.

A Man Called SOMENO

by Andy Smith

Movie Giant Amongst Legends

Having followed the kung fu movie genre from the early '70s, like many others, I developed a fascination for the some of the actors and casts, from that era. Before choosing to go and watch a movie, we firstly would look to see who the stars were. There were many that caught the imagination of the local cinema goers, including the Filipino actor – Tony Ferrar, in his role as Tony Falcon – Agent X-44, followed by those who had featured in the films originating out of the Hong Kong studios, namely Wang Yu, Chen Sing, Bruce Liang, David Chiang, Chen Kwan Tai, to name a few. There were also a number of tough looking characters that appeared mainly as villains or the 'bad guys', who had audiences in uproar during the end fights. YUKIO SOMENO was one of those movie actors, who played a pivotal role in those early films.

Yukio Someno first appeared for Shaw Brother in 1968. He was later involved in a host of other movies during the 1970s, before finishing up his acting role in 1984. In addition to co-starring in forty-four films, his illustrious career in the movie business also included his roles as interpreter, stuntman, producer, martial arts director, assistant action director, production manager and planning.

Someno was born and raised in Koga City, Ibaraki Prefecture, Japan. His practice in karate started at the age of fifteen years old. Although he was also interested in kung fu, this was not a style he knew, nor got involved with during that time.

Before going to work at the Shaw Brothers studios in Hong Kong, he worked as a 'coast guard officer' on the patrol boat 'Muroto', for the Japan Coast Guard Department in Yokohama.

He was later spotted by director Chang Cheh and the Shaw Brothers crew in 1968, whilst they were working on a film set in Japan. He decided to go back with them to Hong Kong, to work on other Shaw movies. In October 2005, Someno conducted and interview, where he gave an insight on how he started out, his journey in the movie business and some of the actors he worked with.

Below, is a text extract from that interview – credits to both Toby Russell and Jiro Chino.

EARLY DAYS AS A COAST GUARD OFFICER

"I started to learn karate when I was fifteen years old, where I studied under Master Kenei Mabuni. I trained every day, and stopped around 1995. I used to train with my good friend Sung Ting Wei. I got into the film industry, well while I was working as a marine police, Shaw Brothers, Chang Cheh and Wang Yu came to Japan to film *Golden Swallow*. That was the first film I was involved in. In those days many actors could not ride a horse, so I used to double for them horseback riding. Chang Cheh said 'This Japanese guy is good' so they brought me to Hong Kong. I later signed up with him. As many actors could not ride, I spent most of the time doubling for them.

"When I first arrived at Shaw Brothers, it was huge and busy studio. There were other Japanese people there too, like the director Umetsugu Inoue and Ko Nakahira, cameraman Yukio Miyagi and Tadashi Nishimoto. There were ten or so Japanese working there. Horsemen, karate men and fighting instructors. So, there were many other Japanese working there, doing their thing. We were very happy at Shaw Brothers and worked there for many years."

His recollection of some of the kung fu stars, that he worked with:
JAMES NAM

"James Nam is a really nice guy. Director Cheng Chang invited him to Shaw Brothers. Actually, James Nam is very good at kung fu. But I only shot two films with him. He has a very warm personality and he will always pay for dinner. Also, he is very serious when it comes to filmmaking. I like him a lot."

LARRY LEE

He was Masfumi Suzuki's student in Karate. He was a 5th Dan in his style. He was also a Karate instructor. The director of Thunderkick loved Kung fu films and he invited Larry to star in the film. They chose me to play the villain. So it was two karate men fighting it out. But since we were both good at karate, it was a real hard hitting fight. The Action Director showed us the moves but in the end we fought it out ourselves. He would block and I would block. It was more like a real fight.

BRUCE LEE AND UNICORN CHAN

In 1971 Bruce Lee came to Hong Kong. I was at Shaw Brothers then. Bruce and Unicorn Chan were visiting the studios, as they arrived by taxi. This was the first time I met Bruce Lee, I had just finished working, and was going to Tsim Sha-tsui for dinner. I saw them waiting by the entrance as I

TRAINING HIS STUDENTS

THE CENTER IS BEN WAI SHIHAN! - HIS STUDENT THAT RUNS THE SCHOOL NOW

THIS IS MR. LAOKARYON WHO TAUGHT ME THE SWORD OF CHINA

drove by. I beeped the car horn and told Unicorn 'hey jump in'.

Unicorn got in along with this other guy, who was Bruce Lee. The two of them rode in my car. Unicorn sat in the front and Bruce sat in the back. Unicorn then introduced me. 'Hey Someno this is Bruce Lee'. I said great and shook his hand. Wow! He had a really strong grip. I thought this guy has got something. Anyway we arrived at Tsim Sha-tsui. I told Unicorn, let's go eat. He agreed and I treated them to Japanese meal. During dinner, he grumbled 'Shaw Brothers are too cheap'. I asked him what he meant by that. He said that Shaw Brothers would not pay $10,000 per film. So I said, why not go to Golden Harvest? Unicorn agreed and later took Bruce to GH, and introduced him to Raymond Chow. Later Raymond hired him."

KURATA SAN

When Yasasuki Kurata first arrived in Hong Kong he knew nothing about filmmaking. He had just graduated from university in Japan and had not studied filmmaking. He came to Shaw Brothers and appeared in two films there. One was *The Angry Guest* and the other I forgot the title. Anyway, I know that he made two films. He was only so-so, and Shaw Brothers did not extend his contract. He had decided to go back to Japan, but as we are from the same prefecture, I told Kurata not to return, but to hang around in Hong Kong and make some films. So I introduced him to Ng See-yuen, who had just had a big hit with the film *Bloody Fists*. I had known Ng See-yuen from when he was an assistant at Shaws, so I introduced him. He was just preparing to shoot a new film called *The Good and the Bad*, so he hired Kurata. I helped out with translating on the set, and also, how to fight in front of the camera.

After *The Good and Bad* was released, Kurata became a million dollar actor. He then went on to appear in *The Rage of the Wind*. I also appeared in that. I was using a samurai sword in the film. Also, that movie was a big hit and Kurata was now a confirmed star.

NINJA AND DRAGONS

The film was a co production between Japan and Hong Kong. Originally, they wanted to use Sanada but went with Junya instead. So we went to China to film. Many Japanese were involved in the production. It was a good experience. They had their own Chinese action director but as we were filming ninja style, they did not know how to choreograph the ninja style properly, so they asked me to come along also. As this movie was a co production between Hong Kong and Japan, we were just paid for our work. As for the success of the film, I'm not clear how well it did. There must have been some agreement between the two companies over territories. This movie was never released in Japan. The Hong Kong company sold it to the rest of the world. So the Japanese public were not aware of this film. I think this is a shame. I was unhappy about this.

THE DIRECTOR OF THE DRAGON NINJA!

MAGNIFICENT BOXER

In a more recent conversation with Someno, he talked a little about some other kung fu movies stars, notably Chen Sing, who sadly passed away in 2019, also Chan Wei Man and Bruce Liang.

CHEN SING

"The most memorable memory of 'Chen Xing' was that he taught a karate instructor at a place called North Point on the Hong Kong side. Near the side of my house, I used to go to his dojo to train, and when I got home, we used to drink coffee with him. He said that 'Someday we'll face each other in a movie!'. This dream came true with Ng See-yuen producer's work *Tora Shimoyama! – Rage of the Wind*. He fought with strength and pride, against me!

BATTLING CHAN WEI-MAN

CHAN WEI-MAN

Chang, Wai, Man (Chen Keito) is a real boxer! At the Korakuen Tournament in Japan, he was the man who knocked out a Japanese boxer in round one. He starred in many movies! He is a man who is very passionate about his work. He was very good in the movie *Bravest Fist*.

BRUCE LIANG

Bruce Liang was a karate instructor, one of Akira Nagata's students, but also a very good kicker. Other than his movies, he is a very polite and very kind man. He had problems with his business for a while, but he made a big comeback by appearing in kung fu films. He gave me five bottles of very expensive wine for my sixtieth birthday celebration! I will never forget it.

FAVORITE ACTRESS

My favorite actress was Li Ching. I did all her horse riding stunts. Unfortunately, she

MRS SIBERT FU, A CLOSE ACTRESS FRIEND

passed away in 2018. I still to this day, remember her smile.

On a personal note, I was fortunate to meet Someno in March 2006, at his birthday celebration, when myself, Dharmesh Patel and Toby Russell attended the International Film Art Exhibition, in Hong Kong. If he ever reads this article, it was a privilege and honour to meet you Someno San!, as well as your star studded guests from the Shaw Brothers studios, and beyond.

Someno San spends almost all of his time these days at home, due to the Covid restrictions. He enjoys going to see his pet Labrador, who his daughter now takes care of. He has never visited Europe, but would like to do so in the future, if it is possible. Also, he looks forward to meeting up with all his friends again in Hong Kong, one day soon. Finally, he wishes everyone the best of health, and the Eastern Heroes magazine, much success.

Yukio SOMENO
Interview

by Simon Prichard
Translated by Jonathan Sparrow.

The story begins in 1948 when Yukio was born to a farming family in Japan. During his childhood he grew fond of horse riding which would later open doors to the Hong Kong film industry.

SP: *Yukio, it sounds like a nice childhood; what memories do you have of this time?*

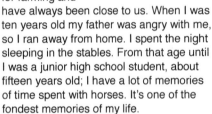

THE HOUSE WHERE YUKIO WAS BORN

WAS A STUDENT BEFORE JOINING THE JAPANESE COAST GUARD

YS: I was born into farming and brought up as a farmer. I have loved horses since I was a young boy. Horses were always necessary for farming and have always been close to us. When I was ten years old my father was angry with me, so I ran away from home. I spent the night sleeping in the stables. From that age until I was a junior high school student, about fifteen years old; I have a lot of memories of time spent with horses. It's one of the fondest memories of my life.

SP: *At 15 years of age, what made you want to start learning martial arts?*

YS: Just before I graduated junior high school, I had the opportunity to see my grandfather performing karate in Tokyo. That was the moment that led me to have an interest in karate.

SP: *You trained under Master Kenei Mabuni 10th Dan. Master Kenei Mabuni is the son of Kenwa Mabuni, the founder of Shito-ryu karate and one of the most important karate practitioners in the history of martial arts. What was your daily training routine and what was sparring like? I can imagine it was tougher than today.*

YS: After I graduated junior high school, I started working in Tokyo. At this time, I started attending Tokyo Oku Dojo. My teacher was Kenzou Mabuni. At this time there were three famous teachers, one was Mabuni Kenwa sensei, another was Mabuni Kenei sensei and the last was my own teach Mabuni Kenzou sensei.

The practice environment was incredibly strict, but my teacher was the only one able to convey to me the mental strength and spirit of the martial art.

SP: *Shaw Brothers directors Chang Cheh and Wang Yu came to shoot* The Golden Swallow *in Japan. How did you get involved with the film?*

YS: The Shaw Brothers production team came to shoot a location in a place called Gotemba, which is near Mount Fuji. At this time, I taught the actor Jimmy Wong how to ride horses. After this the Director Chang Cheh invited me to come to Hong Kong to teach horsemanship to other actors. That is how I ended up in Hong Kong.

At this time, I was working for the coast guard. My ship's name was Muroto. My parents were against me giving up this job and going to Hong Kong, I chose to ignore them and went to Hong Kong.

SP: *As you had rode horses all your life, how was it transitioning to riding horses in films? Did you have to teach the horses to fall for the camera? What horse stunts did you do? Did you ever get hurt?*

YS: In the movies you have to follow the direction that's given and expected for the part. For example, I would be expected to dress as a female actress and ride in a more ladylike fashion for certain scenes. When I was free to ride horses for myself, I would choose to ride without a saddle. I have always found that riding saddleless allows me to connect more with my horse, it allows both the horse and rider to understand each other more.

In order to get the horses to perform the stunts on camera, say falling or an action scene, the most important thing is for the rider and horse to breath as one.

SP: *When you got to Kowloon, Hong Kong, the Shaw Brothers studios were in their heyday. What was it like in the studio? How many film sets did they have? How big was it? Can you please describe what it was like?*

OUTSIDE SHAW BROTHERS

YS: They say the Shaw Brothers were the biggest film studio in Asia at this time. I remember there being about twelve studios, and each one was huge, I was very surprised at that time. The studios were so big they could build an entire forest inside one!

SP: *How did you find fighting Chinese styles? Did any of it have any influence on your fighting style or within your training in Shito-ryu karate?*

YS: Within Chinese martial arts there are a surprising number of fighting styles. For example, Monkey, Praying Mantis, Snake, and Tiger style. There are so many I don't think I could count them all.

Whilst teaching karate in Hong Kong I was asked to fight many times. Regardless of style each person I fought was very strong. Due to me not knowing the techniques my opponents were using I had to rely purely on my own instincts in order to fight. Thanks to these fights I met many people who I call friends today.

No matter how strong or weak I may have thought an opponent to be, the most important thing was to show my opponent's respect.

I was taught Chinese sword fighting, but although interesting I have never let other styles alter my karate. I have however learnt a lot about timing and speed.

SP: *You have worked on some notable films, including* The Heroic Ones *with David Chiang, but one that really stands out is* King Boxer *(aka* Five Fingers of Death*), where you played Oshima Shotaro. Do you have any stories from this film?*

YS: The director asked "Someno-san, please show me some karate," so in front of the staff and director I demonstrated a

THE MAGNIFICENT

WITH CHANG CHEH, 1967

karate kata. When I finished the demonstration the people who had gathered around me gave me a big round of applause, one of these people was the actor James Nam (南宮勲). I was very happy.

SP: *One of your best screen fights, I believe, is* Thunderkill *where you play the Casino boss and the villain. The film also stars James Nam and Bolo Yeung. In the film you fight Larry Lee (Chin-kun Li) a 5th dan karate instructor. How was this and did you have any influence on the choreography?*

YS: I gave my ideas as to how the fight might be played out, but I didn't have any final say in the direction. Larry was from a different school of karate, and showed off his style in the fight, as did I. *Thunderkill* was a big hit in the Philippines!

SP: *One of your final films was* Ninja in Dragon's Den *(1982). This film stars Conan Lee and the now Hollywood actor, Hiroyuki Sanada (John Wick 4 / Mortal Kombat 2021). This film was also Corey Yuen's first credited directorial debut. What was it like working on this set?*

YS: *Ninja in Dragon's Den* was filmed entirely in Taiwan. There were Koreans, Chinese, Taiwanese, and Japanese people involved in the filming.

The multiple languages created a huge problem with communication during filming.

There's a scene in the film in which Hiroyuki Sanada's character cuts off my ear. The audience always laughed at that scene. The scene was filmed after the rain, and it was incredibly easy to slip. It was a tough scene to film. After filming though, everyone got on really well.

PEOPLE RELATED TO BRUCE LEE!

SP: *I have heard that you once went for dinner with your friend Unicorn Chan and his friend, an unknown actor at the time, Bruce Lee. Can you please tell us this story please?*

YS: I met Unicorn in 1968 when I was working at the Shaw Brothers studios. Bruce Lee came to Hong Kong through his connection to Unicorn. Unicorn and Bruce felt that American cinema looked down on them, so they decided to star in Hong Kong movies in order to show what they could do and be taken more seriously as actors. During the time that Unicorn Chan and Bruce Lee were at Shaw brothers the new vice president, Monahon, entered the company and triggered large-scale restructuring. This led to Bruce Lee being unsuccessful in the interview stage at Shaw Brothers. I picked up a depressed looking Unicorn and Bruce in my car after their interview. Because they seemed so down, I took them both to Nagoya restaurant in town, with the intention of making them feel better.

While in the restaurant I suggested to them to try out Golden Harvest, however they were worried about this due to golden harvest being a relatively new company.

THUNDERKILL

THE DRAGON NINJA IS BEING FILMED

When I first shook Bruce Lee's hand I was surprised by the strength of his grip, but I also realized that he was a fellow martial artist.

These are still great memories for me.

SP: Whilst you have starred in many films, which one, or ones, have the fondest memories for you?

YS: The film that holds the fondest memories for me is *The Human Goddess* staring Li Ching, by the Shaw Brothers. I've always wanted to ride a horse like a jockey in a horse race, and during this film I was actually able to ride on the Hong Kong race track like a real Jockey.

SP: Are there any actors or directors that you would have liked to work with? If so, who?

YS: One of the directors I would have liked to work with again is Ho Meng-hua, because thanks to him I was able to realise my own dreams. Whilst working for him doing stunt work for a film in Hong Kong, a documentary was filmed about me on the set.

I would have also liked to have the chance to work with Li Ching one more time.

SP: Whilst you have achieved so much in life, it's not over yet, you wish to write a semi-autobiographical book called Uma to Shonen *(馬と少年) The horse and the boy. Could you please explain what it is about?*

YS: Of course, the book is basically a biography of my youth, which revolves around my life and connection with my pet horse. The book is basically based in reality however I have added some fiction to it, hence semi-autobiographical. It celebrates the fact that were it not for that horse, I would not have had the life I have had led. That horse meant I was able to work in Hong Kong, and then after that continue working with horses throughout my career. I have been truly blessed.

One of the messages I want to pass on through this book, is that if you truly learn to look after and care for your animal, they will in return love and take care of you.

SP: How is your lineage of karate taught today?

YS: Sadly, these days, I no longer practice karate. From around 1968 I was

YUKIO WITH SAMMO

YUKIO WITH JACKIE CHAN

teaching karate in Hong Kong. One of the students I taught at that time, who goes by the name of Ben Wai, is now a karate teacher in Hong Kong. His school is called Hong Kong Shito-ryu Shin-bukai.

SP: Whilst everything in life must move forward, what do you think of the way karate is taught now compared to when you were younger?

YS: In my time it was incredibly strict, and my student Ben Wai, continues to teach in that strict manner.

SP: Is there anything else you would like mention?

YS: Thank you for taking the time to talk to me for this article and thank you to those who have taken the time to read it. I appreciate it immensely.

I'm also very grateful for the time the staff have taken with preparing this interview. Thank you very much.

I don't really have much of an education to speak of, but I always did my best to achieve what I wanted. No matter your own personal situation I truly believe that if you try hard enough you can do anything. 頑張ってください.

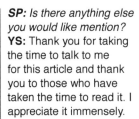

In life you will meet many people, you will encounter both good things and bad, however don't rush things, take your time, and enjoy the stroll.

Be thankful towards people for the things they do.

I'M AN OLD FRIEND AND I WORKED WITH HIM IN MANILA!

Thank you, it has been an honour speaking with you.
貴重な時間と、お話をどうもありがとうございます。

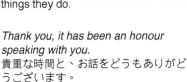

the BADDEST BAD GUY of Them All

by Michael Nesbitt

The GERALD OKAMURA Interview

Gerald Okamura might be one of the most recognizable faces in action movies, with his bald head and long beard, his menacing stare has sent chills down the spines of many so-called action heroes. With over ninety credits to his name, and with a career spanning nearly five decades, Gerald Okamura has probably played a bad guy in more movies than any other actor. By starring in such classics as *Big Trouble in Little China*, *Blade*, *Hot Shots Part Deux*, and *Rapid Fire*, Okamura built up a huge fan base and has become a cult legend throughout the world.

MN: *Can you tell me where and when you were born?*

GO: I was born one day in November 1940, in a small town called Waiakea Houselots (Hilo) on the Big Island (HAWAII), in the Territory of Hawaii.

MN: *What was it like growing up in Hawaii during the 1940s and '50s?*

GO: The 1940s and '50s were awesome fun times for me. It was play/school, most of the time. People back then never locked their cars or their homes, and people trusted each other more. They also looked after each other more. I remember summer time was best with no school or homework. I would meet up with classmates every day and would go swimming and spearfishing (with a homemade speargun). We would go and get 'bento' (box lunch) to eat by the ocean. It was so much different back in the 1940s and '50s than it is today. I was a barefooted kid growing up in a more peaceful world. I only started wearing shoes when I went to High School in 1956.

MN: *Can you tell me when and why you moved to America, and what were your first impressions of America?*

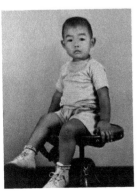

GO: I graduated from Hilo High School in June 1958 and joined the US Army on July 4th, 1958. I was in the 4th All-Hawaii Company. This enlistment was kind of different as it was made up mostly of 1958 High School grads from all the different islands. Each Island made up a platoon. Big Island was the 4th Platoon, and we were presented with 'The Best Platoon' honours for our basic training. I took my basic training at Fort Ord in California. The territory of Hawaii was already part of America so the question is kind of hard to answer. I went from an Island in the middle of the ocean to a large continent, Hilo to Honolulu to California (Fort Ord).

MN: *How did you first get into martial arts?*

GO: My very first martial arts training was in Judo around 1952-53. It was at a Temple in Waiakea (Hilo). We used the basement of the temple for our training (our dojo). I was small as a kid and with me coming from a

and lots of my classmates were there too, and a few older guys that had also joined. I was sent to Schole Field Barracks in Honolulu, to get processed, then we went on a Troop Transport Ship which headed for Oakland, California. It was a bad boat ride for me as I was sick the whole trip (which was four days). There was more processing at Oakland before getting on a bus and heading down to Fort Ord, and that is where I took my basic training. Life during basic training was very basic, especially when we were allotted our toilet paper for the month. By the time you got to the last week of the month, you ran out of toilet paper, so we all had to go to the PX and buy newspapers to substitute for our toilet paper, ha-ha. After finishing up with my basic training I got shipped to Fort Eustis, Virginia, to start my schooling as a fixed wing mechanic. After I graduated from fixed wing mechanic school, I got shipped back to Fort Ord in California. Now I'm crew chief to three L-19 Bird Dogs aircraft, and two TL-19 Trainer Bird Dogs aircraft. When I was down to my last thirteen

Japanese family it was kind of mandatory for me to take up judo. And there were not too many other martial arts around at that time. Sensei Kawasaki taught me judo and he was my very first instructor in the martial arts. I feel that my training in judo was the best thing I did to help me with my martial arts career and helped me build my solid foundation. Later they had included aikido training there, but it was closed-door training. I and other judo guys would find ways to watch their aikido training without them knowing.

I also used to hang out at Waiakea Social Settlement, which was kind of like a YMCA, and they had a gym next to this building. We (my gang), would sleepover at the Settlement on weekends. They had kendo training at the gym during the week and they kept the Kendo equipment at the gym, so on weekends we would borrow the equipment and have our own fights. Those days were awesome fun times for me and my friends.

While in the US Army, I got shipped to Korea on a thirteen-month tour, and it was there that I trained in tae-kwon-do for about twelve months. I was stationed at K46 Wonju, Korea at the time and the airstrip I was assigned to was about five and a half

miles from the K46 Compound, but it had a gym there and that's where we had our tae-kwon-do training. Students were all military people and I used to go five days a week after finishing up my military work at the airstrip.

After getting discharged from the US Army in July 1961, I made my move to California to get schooling as an A&P mechanic. Then one day a salesman came knocking on my apartment door (in Los Angeles, Ca) and it was this salesman that invited me to El Monte, California and this is when I first met Jimmy H. Woo and was introduced to kung fu san soo for the first time.

MN: *Did you do any other sport when you were young?*
GO: Along with doing judo, I also shared my time playing baseball. I played little league baseball and in 1953 we took champs. Then I moved on to pony league baseball and we took champs again in 1954.

MN: *Could you tell us more about your military service?*
GO: I joined the US Army in July 1958, Right after graduating from High School. I was stationed with the 4th All Hawaii Company

months before my discharge, I get orders to go back to Korea, where I got assigned to KMAG (Korean Military Advisor Group). I was supposed to take the boat, but I put in for seven days of leave in Hawaii before I went back to Korea and this meant they had to fly me back, I was so happy about that. And that is how I got assigned to K-46 Wonju. I was a crew chief again but now I had to look after four L-20s and two L-19s. I also had three Korean civilians that did most of the mechanic work for me. When I was finally discharged, they again had me assigned to take the boat for my discharge to Oakland, but I said I wanted my discharge in Hawaii instead, so I got to fly home to Hawaii. Anything to get out of that dreaded boat ride. I was discharged in July 1961 in Hawaii.

MN: What did you do after leaving the Army?

GO: In 1962 I had a forty-hour-a-week job at Douglas Aircraft Company in Santa Monica, California. I was in Development Operations as a jig and fixture builder. Then I went to McDonnell Douglas Aircraft Company in Santa Monica, and then to McDonnell Douglas Aircraft Company in Huntington Beach, and then to Boeing Aircraft Company in Huntington Beach. I had forty-four years working with this aircraft company.

MN: How did you first get into acting?

GO: This kind of came by accident. A gig on the TV series *Kung Fu* would be my first of anything in my so-called acting career. I had my forty-hour-a-week job and I had to find ways to fit my acting gigs in. I did this by saving and using my vacation days to work on all the movie and TV stuff. When I was working at the Aircraft Company, I was training in kung fu san soo in El Monte, California, under Jimmy H. Woo. One day I go to class after finishing work and Jimmy H. Woo calls me over to his desk because he wanted to talk to me. He came straight to the point and says: "I got a call from people from the *Kung Fu* TV series last night and they want to use me for a one-day acting gig, but I don't want to go, as they don't pay me enough. So I want you to go in my place". And not knowing the business, I said: "Okay." Jimmy H. Woo continued telling me: "It is for tomorrow. You report to Warner Bros Studios at 6:30 am." And that was the start of my career as an actor, in Season 1 Episode 8 called *Chains*.

MN: Could you tell us about your experience working on the set of the Kung Fu *TV series?*

GO: Well, the next day I'm there at 6:00am and now I'm inside Stage 7 and I'm looking around to talk to somebody from production. I was lucky as I ran into Mr. David Chow who was the technical advisor, and at that time I did not know him but by name. So I explained to him that Jimmy

THE KUNG FU SAN SOO SCHOOL

H. Woo didn't want the job and he wanted me to take his place. Again, not knowing the business, I didn't know that things don't work that way. But Mr. David Chow saved my bacon and said it was alright for me to replace Jimmy. That was the good part. Now I'm told to report to the Makeup Department right away, so I rush to get there. Then more negative things happened as the makeup lady says to me: "Do you want to shave your head or wear a skull cap?". I did not want to shave my head and I didn't know anything about wearing a skull cap, but I thought the best option was wearing the skull cap, so I went with that. By 7:00am I'm in my skull cap and then I go for my wardrobe. When I'm done in the

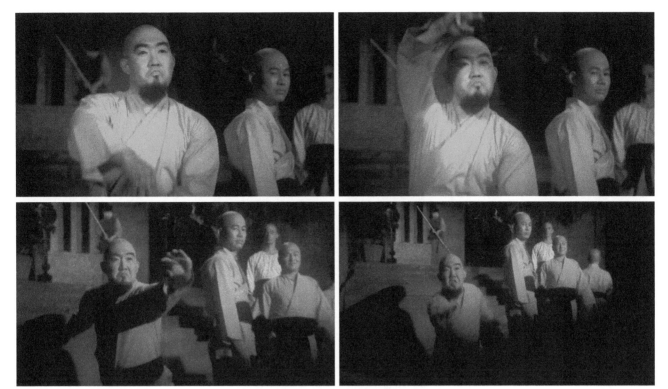

Wardrobe Department, the wardrobe lady says to me: "Okay! You are ready for the camera, go hang out by Craft Service and have a coffee and Danish". I didn't shoot my scene until around 7:30 pm that night. I thought to myself, 'what a way to break into Show Business'. When this episode aired on TV on March 8, 1973, I told many people that I was going to be on that night. At the time, the early 1970s, the *Kung Fu* TV series was very popular, but to my disappointment, it ended up being a very quick scene. But hey, that's Show Business. I didn't get to shoot any scenes with David Carradine, but I did with his brother Keith, as he was playing the young Kwai Chang Caine, and he was a great actor. However, I did get to work with David many years later on a different project.

MN: *You were in the James Caan 1975 classic,* The Killer Elite, *could you tell us about that?*
GO: *The Killer Elite* was the very first movie I worked on. It was on this project that I had to join SAG (Screen Actors Guild). I carried around a letter that Sam Peckinpah (the director) gave me, and this is what helped me join SAG. We had an awesome cast of big named actors on the set of the movie, including James Caan, Mako, Bo Hopkins, Robert Duvall, and Burt Young. I had to audition for it with the director. I got a phone call from one of my fellow black belts from Kung Fu San Soo. He tells me that he got an audition for a martial arts movie, and he wanted to borrow some of my weapons for this audition. I told him that I go with my weapons as I don't loan them out to anyone just in case, I don't get them back. To my surprise, he says: "Okay, you and I can go as a team." So we go and

audition for Sam Peckinpah, and he picks both of us to work in the movie. I had to fly up to San Francisco, as one of the locations was at the San Francisco Airport, the other location was at the Mothball Fleet in Suisun Bay. Sam Peckinpah was one of only two directors that called me by my first name. The other being John Carpenter. I had a scene with Burt Young (from the *Rocky* movies), and he was carrying a gun in his

hand and during our small fight scene, he backhands me while still holding the gun in his hand. His hand was supposed to make contact with the back of my head, but I got hit with the butt of the gun instead. I went down and I started seeing stars, and not the Hollywood type either, ha-ha. Back at San Francisco Airport, I read the script and it called for us to try and knock off some good guys. I am wearing an arm cast, and I conceal a stainless-steel tube in it, specifically for a blowgun. My darts for the blowgun were made of a .046 DIA stainless steel welding rod with plastic balls taken from some cheap jewellery. I could go undetected through airport security with the stainless-steel weapon. But I never got to use the weapon on screen because production said the darts were not big enough, and wouldn't show up on film.

MN: *You got to work with Chuck Norris on the 1980 movie* The Octagon, *what was Chuck like to work with?*
GO: I never actually got to shoot any scenes with Chuck, but I knew Chuck

from doing martial arts. But for me, working on a Chuck Norris movie was an honour. I already had so much respect for him as a talented martial artist and a gentleman's gentleman. I was also honoured to be working with Aaron Norris, Chuck's brother, and stunt coordinator on *The Octagon*. But for me, the biggest honour working on this movie was when I first met Richard Norton. A super nice guy and a very talented martial artist. We don't see each other much these days, but we still call each other friends.

MN: In 1985 you appeared in one of my favourite childhood TV series, Knight Rider, *could you tell us about that?*
GO: This is another TV project I was glad to add to my resume. I didn't have a character role, I just worked on the project as a stuntman. I had a chance to meet David Hasselhoff and talked to him in-between takes. Sometimes at the Craft Service table for coffee. He was always ready to take photos with people if they were watching us shooting scenes at a location. One day while we were at the Craft Service table drinking coffee, he told me: "You have to take care of the people (Fans) because they are the ones that keep you and your show going on".

Another TV series I worked on was *MacGyver*. I worked on it as a stuntman. I also worked on an early TV series called, *A Man Called Sloane*. I was new to the business, and I was super happy to work on this project because of Robert Conrad who starred in the *Wild Wild West* TV series. But it was a big disappointment when I met him as he was not a very nice person. I think he would be the only person in show business I didn't like. Another TV series was *Gavilan* with Robert Urich. It didn't run for very long, they only made thirteen episodes before it got cancelled, but the episode I worked on was special for me. I was just a stuntman, but it was a special stuntman role because I played a Yakuza, and that meant tattoos. It was a very early call time, something like 4:00am at the studio to get all of us covered with tattoos. It was another fun project because I was working with so many martial artists/stunt people who were friends.

MN: In 1986 you acted in your most iconic role as one of the henchmen in the classic movie, Big Trouble in Little China. *Could you tell us how you got the role?*
GO: WOW! Where do I start? It all started on a cold windy day, with thunder, lightning, and rain, with the sun shining bright in the southern California sky. I heard of an open call/audition at the 20th Century Fox studio for a movie project called *Big Trouble in Little China* and they were looking for a lot of martial artists. So I went and took one of

ON THE SET OF GAVILAN WITH ROBERT URICH

my students to throw around, just to show John Carpenter (the director) my martial arts skills. I also took with me some of my weapons to show him that I could also use weapons to fight with. They did not tell you on the spot if you got the job or not, so I left and went home. That night I got a call from one of the co-ordinators saying that

they wanted to use me on this movie project. He wanted me to report to the 20th Century Fox Prop Department the next morning. My name would be at the gate to the studio lot so I could drive my car straight in and drive directly to the prop department. I get there early the next morning and report to the prop department and give them my name. I told them I was told to report there, and I would find out what kind of props the production team wanted me to use for the character I was going to play in the movie. The prop guy comes out from the back room and hands me two gold-plated six-shooters (handguns) with pearl handles and another guy hands me the double gun holsters. Man was I surprised! The guy then says: "Wait we are not done yet. John Carpenter wants you to wear two bandoliers, loaded with extra bullets that only fit a large rifle." I have to thank John Carpenter for giving and making me this character, as it became my most iconic image. On July 2nd, 2021, we celebrated the 35th Anniversary of our movie. Many fans all around the world have given the movie life. And this character that John Carpenter made me into, also found life.

I have a little story to share with you on how I celebrated the 35th Anniversary of the *Big Trouble in Little China* movie. I had some help from a brewing company. I got in touch with Eureka Heights Brewing Company in Houston, Texas, to see if they could help me celebrate the 35th Anniversary of the movie and to my surprise, they said: "OK, let's do it." The first thing was to develop a beer (this company has a tap room with all kinds of different types of beer and ale, the room also had a large Titan screen TV in there). The crew and I at Eureka were busy developing this ale for the previous few months, so we would be ready to drop this

surprise on July 16, 2021. So on that date, the Eureka Brewing Company had a watch party and dropped the surprise ale called Golden 6 Shooter Ale. We also had the *Big Trouble in Little China* movie playing on the big Titan screen TV for all that came to the party. It was a great way for me to celebrate the 35th Anniversary of the movie.

MN: What were Kurt Russell and Kim Cattrall like to work with?

GO: I did not have the good luck to talk much with Kurt Russell or Kim Cattrall on the set, mainly because I didn't have one on one scenes with them. But from what I saw of them both, they both seemed to be wonderful people. I did get to meet them and say a fast hello and even a quick handshake from both of them. I didn't have a character role in this movie project, I went in as a stuntman/martial artist, so I hung out with the rest of the stuntmen/martial artists rather than the main actors. They also had about 75 to 80 martial artists onset as background people, and it became a really fun project as I got to work with lots of my friends.

MN: Could you tell us a story or two from the set of Big Trouble in Little China*?*

GO: We were shooting on the 20th Century Fox Studio lot, so Production does not have to feed us lunch. We are on our own. So it all started with the guys from Hawaii. We didn't want to eat at the 20th Century Fox commissary, and we didn't want to go outside the studio to eat lunch, so all of us Hawaii guys decided to bring in food, which we called Potluck. That was awesome and fun and also a chance to talk story with all the others. That small group of guys didn't stay small for long, yes, the food was that good, ha-ha. The only thing missing was the sandy beaches and the ocean. We had all different kinds of food, and it was hard to go back to work right after lunch, as we were always so full. We had to find out before lunch who was working on the first scene

after lunch as those guys had to have a light lunch.

One day I got to meet Goldie Hawn, the partner of Kurt Russell. When we were shooting a group scene and Kurt Russell was in it with us, Goldie showed up onset. She was sitting with Kurt, so I went over to say hello to her and shake her hand. She

was a wonderful funny lady. And she laughed the same as she does in her movies.

MN: You appeared in something a little different when you acted in an episode of Falcon Crest*, as Mr. Ito in 1987. How did that come about and what was it like working onset?*

GO: I didn't work any scenes with the big stars of *Falcon Crest*. The character role of Mr. Ito was supposed to be a recurring role, but I guess I didn't do a good enough job, so they only had me on that one episode. The usual way of looking for work is, my agent would call me to say I had a 1:00 pm appointment/audition at wherever and for which character. Usually, I had to take time off from work to do these interviews. Then after the interviews, I go back to work and wait for a call from my agent, (if I got the job or not, more not than got).

MN: You had the starring role in the 1989 underground classic movie, Ninja Academy*, could you tell us about that?*

GO: This movie is very special in so many different ways. Yes! It was a starring role, but I was also on the poster, and I thought that was awesome. I didn't use my agent on this project because I didn't have one at that time. My audition was with the director Nico, who also wrote the script. I booked this gig and when the other character roles got booked, we had a group read at the director's house. Some of the other cast members were having a very hard time with the director, but for whatever reason, I had it nice and easy working with him. I didn't know any of the other cast members before this project, but we had James Lew as the stunt co-ordinator, who I did know before this project. And like other projects, we had lots of stunt/martial arts guys that I knew, so again it was great fun working with them. At times we had the chance to put our two cents in, to help the scenes. I thought this movie had a chance to be more successful than it was.

MN: *Is it true that you are the only martial arts kung fu bad guy to appear in illustrious* Vogue *magazine?*

GO: I don't know if it's true or not depending on what you say about being the only martial art Kung Fu Bad Guy to appear in *Vogue* magazine, but maybe back when I first did this project, it could be true. This was my first print job, and I did it without even knowing there was such a thing called a print modelling Job. I was at the Santa Monica Pier shooting a movie called *The Power Within* with TJ Roberts, it was also Art Camacho's first directorial job. I was standing around on the pier in-between takes and watching others shooting their scenes, when this guy walks up to me and asked me if I would be nice enough to take a few photos with this beautiful lady (she had an overcoat on and I later found out under the overcoat all she had on were sexy babydoll clothes). I told the guy I need to check with the director, so I go over to where Art Camacho was shooting and explain to him what had just happened, he then said it was okay for me to do it, and so I did. And that was the start of my modelling career, ha-ha. After taking a bunch of pictures with this sexy lady, the guy said to me: "This photo shoot is for *Vogue* magazine, is there anything I can do for you to repay you for your help?" So I told him just to send me a few pictures and a copy of *Vogue*. The photographer turned out to be a famous photographer from the UK.

After this photoshoot, I go back to my trailer and I'm talking to the makeup girl, and she was the one that told me about the photographer being famous and from the UK. Then three days later, I get a phone call from a lady who says she had a studio, and this photographer was using it while he was in Los Angeles, and she tells me that the photographer wants to schedule me for a photoshoot at her studio. I agreed, so the next day I turn up at the studio. Two days later I get a call from this lady again and now she is telling me that the photographer wants to use one of the pictures for $xxx amount. I didn't know how much they were worth, so I asked the lady if that was okay and she tells me I can ask for any amount I want, and she would relay the information back to the photographer. Well, I asked for too much so there was no deal. But the story does not end here. A few months later a martial artist friend of mine was in the UK and when he came back to Los Angeles, he called me and asked if I did a photoshoot for Armani, because he saw a poster with me on it when he was in the UK. I made it around the world as a model, however, my modelling career was a short one, but it was fun while it lasted.

MN: *You got to work with the amazing Brandon Lee and Dolph Lundgren in* Showdown in Little Tokyo*. What was it like working onset with both of them?*

GO: I was very lucky to be in the same scene with both Brandon and Dolph in the movie, however, I didn't have much interacting with both guys on this project. I went to the audition for the character role of Hagata the Torturer but did not get it. A few days later I was at work at McDonnell Douglas Aircraft Company in Huntington Beach, and while I was on my second shift, I get a call around 10:30pm from the casting lady (the same lady at my audition) and she told me that the actor that got the part was not available the day/night, so they had to move location and shoot something else instead). They were at a location in Long Beach, California for a 6:00am call time, and it was raining, and so they could not shoot any outdoor scenes. So that's why the production team decided to move to a new location to shoot indoors at a brewery plant. So I get this phone call at 10:30pm and she offers me the part and tells me that my call time is for 1:00am. So that is how I was lucky to be in that part of the movie, where I torture both Brandon and Dolph. I ended up with a three-day gig with lots of overtime. I thought Brandon Lee was awesome in this movie, and both guys were gentlemen.

MN: *Were you a fan of Brandon's father Bruce Lee, and did he talk about him much?*

GO: Who is not a fan of Bruce Lee? I have much respect for Bruce but maybe not like most of his fans. He was a thinker and I like the concept of how he would utilise all aspects of all the different kinds of martial arts in the world and make it fit into his own system. He also helped introduce martial arts to the United States TV and movie industry. I can easily be a fan of Brandon Lee as well. Why? Brandon tried to be Brandon Lee and not Bruce Lee. The few times I got to speak with Brandon, he didn't talk much about his father.

MN: *Do you have a story you could tell us about working on the set of* Showdown in Little Tokyo*?*

GO: As we got began shooting my scene, we got to the part of the script that called for the Torturer to work his electrical machine. As we were rehearsing the scene, Dolph Lundgren yells out to the director that he and Brandon couldn't see when I turned the machine on. So I yell back at the director and showed him my idea of how we can make it work. I shout "KIAA" as I turn the switch on the machine and I "KIAA" again when I turn it off. The director liked my idea and asked Dolph and Brandon if that was okay, of course, both of them said it was. I got another payday when they called me to go in for some ADR (Automated Dialogue Replacement) work, and I did my "KIAAs" a few more times and got paid for another full day's work. NICE!!!

MN: *In 1992 you got to work with Brandon Lee again, this time in* Rapid Fire*. Do you have any stories from the set of the movie?*

GO: My second movie project with Brandon was awesome, and in this movie, I have a scene where I fight Brandon. It was Leo Lee (stuntman) and I that fought Brandon. It started with Brandon swinging down on a bag of clothes and knocking Leo Lee, who was guarding two people inside the office, through the glass plate window. Then Leo jumped back out of the office and onto Brandon, now Leo and I are fighting against Brandon. The three of us co-ordinated the fight routine ourselves. At one point Brandon does a crescent kick to my head and I go through the window (no glass). Two movies with Brandon, and two scenes with Brandon, and I knew for certain that Brandon was on his way up, and he did it his own way and I liked the way he was going about it. For some reason, I felt an immediate friendship with Brandon, even when I didn't socialize with him. He was very friendly on the set and always a gentleman.

MN: Brandon died not long after completing Rapid Fire, *how did you hear about his death, and what was your reaction?*
GO: You know something, I cannot remember how and when I heard about the accident. But I do remember being in shock. I didn't go around looking for answers, I just waited to hear what happened. Brandon left us far too soon. RIP Brandon Lee, my friend.

MN: You are known for making your own martial arts weapons, could you tell us how that came about and what kind of weapons you invented.
GO: I bought a pair of sai from a martial arts supply store. That was my very first martial arts weapon, but the prongs were too small/tight for my hands, and it was the kind of casting that you could not adjust. There were not too many martial arts weapons around at that time, so I decided to make my own pair of sai and that was the very first martial arts weapon I made for myself. As the years went by, I got interested in designing weapons for movies and TV, but I also liked collecting different kinds of weapons. Some of the weapons I designed and fabricated got used in TV and movie projects, and I guess

for me, my Okamura hook swords would be the number one weapon that I designed. I got to use them in Eric Lee's *Weapons of Death* movie, and I had them with me for lots of photoshoots for various martial arts magazines.

MN: You appeared in one of the best scenes in Charlie Sheen's 1993 movie Hot Shots Part Deux, *could you tell us about that?*
GO: This movie has become one of my favourite projects to work on, as I had a super character role as the corrupt referee in the fight between Charlie Sheen and James Lew. The most terrible thing on the set of the movie for

me, was when they came to talk to me and told me I had to go get a head made, because at one point in the fight Charlie Sheen and James Lew attack each other with flying kicks and my head ends up in-between their feet. Getting the fake head made caused a lot of problems for me. At one point the guys making the fake head had to make a cast of my real head and cover it with some kind of stuff, and I'm a very claustrophobic person, so it was a struggle, but I got through it in the end. And I'm glad I did because my part in the movie was awesome.

It took many days to shoot this whole scene because it had many special gigs in the script. At one point while shooting the scene, Charlie Sheen was to punch a guy in the face through the wooden ladder, breaking one of the runs of the ladder, at the same time I'm getting up after just getting knocked to the ground. As Charlie continues, he attacks me with a back fist to my jaw, however, he wasn't supposed to make contact, but he did. After the director called cut, Charlie Sheen was the first one to check on me to see if I was okay. But the 200-background people on the set started yelling: "KICK HIS ASS, REF", ha-ha. All in the life of a stuntman. Another special thing that happened in this movie, which was great, happened the day after shooting the fight scene. The producer came to see me and thanked me for a great shoot. I guess he enjoyed all the silly dumb things I was doing on the set.

MN: *You starred alongside Christopher Lambert and Robin Shou in the 1995 movie,* Mortal Kombat, *what are your memories of that movie?*

GO: Quite a few martial artists went to the audition of this one, and when I got a call from Pat Johnson, the fight coordinator, he told me to bring some of my weapons along, as they might use some of them in the movie. So that night, I put together a double crescent weapon and decided to take it along to show Pat at my audition the next day. It was put together really quickly because I wanted to show them a different kind of weapon, and if this design got picked the prop department could copy it to use in this movie. To my surprise, they liked it, and it got picked to be used in the movie, and they used them as they were, they just added a little staining to make them look old. Even stranger, I ended up using them for my character in the movie, and I got to fight one of the main good guys, Robin Shou. My character role was that of an Outworld Warrior, and my soul was saved and stored under the manhole cover in the Black Tower, along with a few other warriors. One of the other warriors in the group was none other than Mr. Fumio Demura. Fumio is a well-known Japanese master of karate, and he was Pat Morita's martial arts stunt double in the *Karate Kid* movies.

MN: *What was it like working with Wesley Snipes in the movie* Blade?

GO: I enjoyed working on this movie as it was the first time, I met Wesley Snipes. I played the part of one of the 13 Elders. While waiting to go onset, I was hanging out by the trailers and talking to Wesley Snipes' bodyguard, who I knew as a fellow martial artist. A few other Elders were hanging out with us, and during one of our talks, I told him that I had never met Wesley before. He then tells me that Wesley Snipes was in his trailer getting ready to go onset, and he said that he would introduce me to him when he came out. A few minutes later Wesley comes out of his trailer with about six other people (make-up, hair, wardrobe, etc) and when he gets to about twelve feet from me, the bodyguard calls out to Wesley telling him that I wanted to meet him. Wesley stops in his tracks and faces me. He looks directly at me, with his feet together and then bows. I return this gesture. He then walks over to me and shakes my hand then steps back again and bows once more and then walks off to go onset. Now comes the best part. The other actors playing Elders are so confused and start yelling at me: "He is the star of this movie and he bowed to you? Who are you?" Then they call us to report to the set. So all us Elders are walking towards the set, and we all run into Wesley walking back to his trailer. When we get within 10-12 feet of him, he stops and bows to

me again. I return this gesture and then we carry on walking towards the set. The other Elders just looked at me confused as to why Wesley showed me so much respect.

MN: *You also were in the movie GI Joe: The Rise of Cobra in 2009. What was it like working on the set?*

GO: I had the character role as the Hard Master. This character is in the comic books and cartoon TV series. In this movie, it is the Hard Master that trains Storm Shadow and Snake Eyes when they are about ten or twelve years old. We never shot any scenes with the main characters of the movie, as we were the flashback parts of the script. So the days when we shot, we were the main characters. The young Storm Shadow was played by Brandon Soo Hoo and the young Snake Eyes was played by Leo Howard. Again the Production needed about eighty background people, and they also needed about forty kids, so they went to get them from martial art schools around the area.

ON SET OF GI JOE

MN: *Is there anyone you wished you could have worked with, but never got the chance?*

GO: The list is far too many to mention. My wish list is very big, but the already worked with list is just as big. Sometimes the B-listers of people I worked with on many different projects, bring back many fond memories for me. You would think the names on the A-listers would be number one. But when I go back and look at my movie career, I couldn't ask for more. Then again, maybe I could, ha-ha. Let me name a couple from the B-listers that I loved working with. One was Marilyn Chambers

(*Angel of H.E.A.T*). And then there is Julie Strain (*Fit to Kill, Dallas Connection, Day of the Warrior,* and *Return to Savage Beach*). They were both great to work with and sadly no longer with us. RIP.

MN: Out of all the movie and TV work you have done, which is your favourite and why?

GO: This is another hard question to answer because all of my TV or movie work is a favourite for different reasons. You would think that *Big Trouble in Little China* would be my number one choice, and you would be correct, but *Showdown in Little Tokyo* would also be my favourite but for different reasons. Maybe *Weapons of Death* or *Ninja Busters* or *Master Demon* would be favourites because these are all Eric Lee movie projects. So, in reality, I have many favourites. You could also ask the question, what do I like best, TV or movies. Well, I guess I need to answer this question and not beat around the bush. *Big Trouble in Little China* is my favourite movie because the movie is still very popular with people all over the world, and it is what I am probably known for the most. The best part of all this madness is that the fans are having fun, and they even have a group on Facebook with 58,000 *Big Trouble in Little China* fans. The fans all over the world have kept my character, the Golden Six Shooter Wing Kong Warrior, alive for thirty-five years. Yes! Thank you to all of you all around the world. Without all of you, none of this would happen.

MN: Which actor or actress did you like working with the most?

GO: These last few questions are really hard for me to answer because each choice has different reasons. But for me the number one actor or actress I liked working with the most would be Julie Strain. I worked on four movie projects with Julie, and three out of the four movies we were partners. All of these movies were with the Andy Sidaris Production Group. I first met Julie when I worked on the 1993 movie *Fit*

to Kill, when I was just a stuntman. Then the next time we worked together was on the movie *The Dallas Connection*. We were a couple of bad guys in that one, and both of us died in the movie. The one after that was, *Day of the Warrior*, and Julie and I come back as the good twins from the previous movie. In the last movie, *Return to Savage Beach*, we play the same character parts. It was a hell of a ride, and I will remember it all forever with very fond memories.

MN: Finally, what does the future hold for Gerald Okamura?

GO: Maybe a starring role as the romantic lead in a blockbuster action movie, fingers crossed, ha-ha-ha-ha.

Please visit Gerald Okamura's official website where you can purchase signed memorabilia:
www.geraldokamura.com

a Jackie Chan GHOST STORY

The Curse of Jackie Chan

by Thorsten Boose
October 2021

When something bad happens to famous people who have done amazing things in their lives and thus inspired countless people, the first thought is often: "Why him/her? It always hits the good guys."

It is hardly noticeable with unknown people, of course. And that even, let's say, personalities who tend to have a negative attitude towards life are being tackled, is shown by plenty examples from world political and military history. Somehow the universe is balancing.

When it comes to Bruce Lee, the sometimes unbelievable stories of the Hong Kong film legend pile up. Even already during his lifetime. His extravagant training methods, his taboo-breaking lifestyle and the philosophical being behind this charming person are just a few factors that make him an extraordinary person to this day.

Where some find inspiration and motivation, others try to crawl deep into an imaginary rabbit hole to collect breadcrumbs for their hungry conspiracy theories. Was Bruce Lee murdered? Are the triads behind it? And was the Lee family really cursed?

We know that we don't know anything. But let's develop one of these theories together and even link it to another Hong Kong film legend: Jackie Chan. Because let's be honest, that's the stuff films can be made of.

Celebrity talks ghosts in show

The year is 1989. Jackie Chan's latest flick is the expensive produced gangster film *Miracles*, in which the enchanting Anita Mui, who is currently being honoured with a biopic at the worldwide box office, shows off her singing skills as a 1930s show act in Shanghai. Jackie is a guest on the popular Hong Kong *Celebrity Talk Show* and joins hosts James Wong, Chua Lam and Ni Kuang.

It is the last episode of the second season. Jackie is sitting in a good mood on a comfortable leather sofa in this '80s scenery and talks about his time on the stage in the 1960s. Even if Jackie is neither religious nor very superstitious, he turns into a storyteller when suddenly a ghost story occurs to him. A ghost story that happened to him himself.

Jackie tells in this interview:

"It was in 1979 in South Korea at the Hing Chow Hotel in Seoul, an upscale hotel at the time. I had a tight schedule with *The Fearless Hyena* and *The Young Master*."

We will come back to this point later. In any case, it was a turbulent time for Jackie and relaxing hours were rather rare. That one night, he explains, he was fast asleep on the bed, on his back, face up. To the right of his bed was a door that led into the spacious bathroom of his suite. There was a full-length mirror opposite the bathroom door.

have a certain picture in mind? Despite this mysterious night encounter, Jackie remained calm.

"It went on for a while. The ghost stood over me, staring straight at me. I didn't know if I was awake or still asleep, so I tried to look around. I could hardly move! But it occurred to me that I was in South Korea," the actor continues to tell. "I just asked the ghost in Korean who it was."

Loud laughter on the *Celebrity Talk Show*, but at this point it should be remembered that it is better not to ask questions that cannot be bared. The ghost woman responded. She slowly knelt in front of Jackie and noiselessly reached out her hand to his head. Even the fearless hyena was frightened then. Jackie tried to escape the ghost woman, as he said, but his body was paralyzed. She got closer and closer, it got darker and darker and then... Jackie fell asleep again.

When he woke up it was morning in Seoul and the sun was shining through his curtains. He said to himself, "It was just a dream. That must have been a bad dream." Confused, the soon-to-be film legend sat on the edge of his bed until he returned to his tight schedule shortly afterwards. But two years later he was to get another visit.

Korean ghosts, take two

According to his descriptions, Jackie was again in South Korea, this time in the Chiu Sin Hotel. He was there with his manager Willie Chan, his friend and colleague Eric Tsang and his then already hated director Lo Wei. All four checked into this hotel. Willie and Jackie shared a room. To be completely honest, one of Willie's later tasks was to always wake his protégé in good time in the morning.

South Korea, early evening, hotel room inside. Jackie is sleeping on the bed. Willie does managerial stuff. Jackie stretches all fours out in a relaxed manner. Suddenly, he wakes up and even scares Willie. The suite is shrouded in subdued light and yet he sees it again, the ghost. The same graceful figure, wrapped entirely in white clothes, her black hair hanging from her head like a curtain and again covering her face. And action!

Jackie explains in the interview, standing there in the middle of the room and staring at him, this time he immediately panicked. Eventually, he began to hyperventilate. He screamed in almost perfect Korean again in fear, "Why are you chasing me? What do you want?" and trembled all over. A cold sweat broke out. But the ghost did not move.

Willie got a shock – because of Jackie, not because of the ghost, because he couldn't see it. He shook Jackie and tried to calm him down. No chance. The star ran out of the room in a panic, down the hall, into the lobby and probably a long

"You know, I sleep deeply at night, but restlessly. It may be that I wake up turned 180 degrees the next morning," the guest explains to the hosts.

This time he actually woke up in the middle of the night and tried to orientate in the room when he slowly began to feel uncomfortable. It felt like someone was still in the room with him. As soon as he grabbed that thought he recognized a person. A ghost stood right next to his face, he stared at the confused Jackie and slowly leaned down to him.

Jackie describes the ghost as a female who wore a white dress and had long black hair that covered her face. Do you already

way further. When he came back he couldn't remember his room number. Willie then found the terrified Jackie wandering somewhere in the hallway and brought him back and finally to calm.

"You know, that was early in the evening, the sun was still shining," Jackie tells the show hosts. "Days later I approached a few locals, we talked about ghosts, and they told me that there are a lot of ghosts in Korea. Many people there believe in ghosts. There are good and bad ones."

The Koreans prayed for him that he saw a good ghost. At this point, Jackie emphasizes twice in the interview that he felt the effects of these disturbing encounters up to the shooting of *Dragon Lord*. And this third incident could at least clear up a few curiosities.

A phone call from beyond?
Actually, Jackie Chan's second Golden Harvest production *Dragon Lord* has nothing to do with ghosts. But even during the shooting in 1981 he was not spared from apparition. For the third time he was in a hotel room, this time he was dozing when he suddenly heard someone say his name.

"Where are you?", he yelled in less hopeful anticipation for the woman in white.

A breeze brushed his face, and he froze. But he was also annoyed. And then he said to himself that he should just relax now. He tried that, but a second breath of wind made his body freeze again, as he describes it. Plus, the constant whispering of his name. At some point he wrested himself from this invisible force and addressed a quick prayer to the gods.

When the budding superstar reported the incident to his friends at Golden Harvest on the set of *Dragon Lord* the next day, they wanted to accompany him to the hotel in the evening as emotional support. But Big Brother declined with thanks. As soon as he arrived at the hotel, the security service explained that there had been a power failure in his suite and that he had to move to another room.

Seriously? Is there a conspiracy going on here? Jackie was annoyed, declined with thanks, but had concerns. The *blindwütige Drachenheld* (German TV title of *Dragon Lord*, translated as 'mad dragon hero') actually got himself a flashlight, showered in the semi-darkness and sang loudly to himself to drive away the maybe evil spirits. At this point in the film you would experience the hero's nervous breakdown and wonder how he'll get out of it.

"It was always in bed! Whenever I went to sleep, the ghost came," Jackie says half-jokingly. "I lay down in the dark and heard the whisper again. I couldn't see it exactly, but I had enough and shouted 'AAH!'"

James Wong, Chua Lam and Ni Kuang obviously had fun during the season finalé of their talk show. So did Jackie, and so he goes on to explain that the vague murmur seemed to be coming from the wall across the room. He tried to make out the area in the dark where the noise was coming from when he widened his eyes – there were sparks coming from the wall!

The wiring in the wall was damaged by the power failure and there was still some residual voltage on the telephone socket, which sparkled. And so Jackie's prejudiced psyche turned a simple electric hiss into an eerie "I died miserably" of an invisible undead in his hotel room.

That was too much even for Chan, the man. He asked for another suite and tried to catch up on some restful sleep. This last weird encounter led Jackie to seriously reconsider the ghost issue. From then on he no longer wanted to believe in paranormal things, he banished these thoughts from his mind. Since then, as far as Jackie lets us know, there have been no further encounters with the ghost woman in white clothes.

The woman in white

Admittedly, a good ending is still missing for a full-length film here. Does the ghost come back after thirty years? Did our film hero just imagine it and if so, why? Or is this actually the curse of Bruce Lee that passed on to Jackie Chan?

In any case, Jackie Chan really shared the stories with the public on the *Celebrity Talk Show* in 1989. But what had he really seen then? What happened to him? Fact is, it took him away, at least for a short time. He broke a sweat and saw things he didn't know were real or not. Really questionable in terms of health.

The figure he saw in 1979 and described in an interview ten years later should be familiar to almost every film lover today. A young woman or a petite person, all in white, with raven-black hair up to her legs that cover her face. You immediately think of horror films like *The Ring* or *Ju-On*.

But the nowadays popular horror figure comes from ancient myths that even exist worldwide. The woman in white has been sighted all over the world for many centuries, including Europe. In the Asian region, mainly in Japan, China and Korea, the described form is very well known.

In Japanese there is the name Onryō, an angry vengeful god who comes from Shintoism. In China there are the so-called Jiangshi, which means something like undead. The Chinese Jiangshi come from a folk tale and look more like stiff zombie vampires. Good to see in films like *Mr. Vampire* or *Encounter of the Spooky Kind*. We'll come back to Yuen Wah's performance in *The Black Tavern* later.

Such beings are also known in Korea. Here they are known as Gwisin. The Gwisin fit Jackie's description very well, because their appearance looks exactly like that. The long black hair that covers the face is typical of Gwisin. The vernacular attributes some properties to them: They can appear to fulfil something unfinished in their life. As an outsider, you are usually only a silent witness of brief paranormal experiences. But they can also appear and move things, either to consciously scare someone or to take revenge on someone.

There are many other different mythological beings, especially in the Far East, who have such properties and manifestations. Basically, to Jackie the woman in white appeared, as we know her from horror films today. But the question still remains: why?

Conscience, triads and an old superstition

In the interview, Jackie says that his first apparition in 1979 was between *The Fearless Hyena* and *The Young Master*. Since memories go back a long time and he sometimes seems to contradict each other in the course of the narrative, one could also infer 1978. At one point he mentioned that he only made ghost-related films for a long time. That definitely falls into the era around *Spiritual Kung Fu*, a kung fu comedy in which five ghosts teach Jackie certain fighting techniques.

The film was shot in mid-1978 and was released in theatres in late November of that year. *Spiritual Kung Fu* was filmed in South Korea, as was *To Kill with Intrigue*, *Snake & Crane Arts of Shaolin* and *Dragon Fist*. All from that era. That explains the two years Jackie claims to have spent in South Korea.

When ghosts became increasingly popular in kung fu films in the late 1970s, Jackie's friend Sammo Hung also took up the topic and made it popular. In 1980, his horror kung fu comedy *Encounter of the Spooky Kind* was released, which triggered a veritable ghost and vampire boom in Hong Kong. The film series *Mr. Vampire* is another example from the golden '80s.

Here, the audience sees the Jiangshi, the zombie-like vampire demons who can only hop around. They are also in *Fantasy Mission Force* from 1983. At the time of the interview, the *A Chinese Ghost Story* franchise was also very popular (hmm, did all of this inspire Chua Lam, one of the hosts, to act as the presenter for *Erotic Ghost Story* in 1990?).

Jackie goes on to say that he had an apparition again two years after the first incident. According to his calculations, it should have been 1981, but by then he was almost rid of Lo Wei and spent millions of HK dollars on his second Golden Harvest

production *Dragon Lord*. I'm more likely to assume that it was the second incident that Jackie describes with the one in 1979, because that was when the drama about Lo Wei's dubious contract extension took place, which would challenge not only him, but also the entire Hong Kong film industry for years.

Lo Wei cheated Jackie back then by changing the blank contract in his favour. He already had Jackie's signature. During the shooting of *The Fearless Hyena 2* in 1979, a dispute broke out when he realized that Lo Wei's system could cost him his career. He packed his things and just ran away.

That started a whole bunch of things: First, Jackie's guilty conscience for not fulfilling a contract. What his father always preached to him "You have to fulfil a contract", so he indirectly betrayed his father as well. He put his manager Willie in trouble, who was extremely committed to his protégé. Lo Wei, a well-known member of the Sun Yee-on gang, a Chinese triad, sent his people after him. They were supposed to bring him back.

Then there was a former Chinese star who indirectly merged Jackie and Seasonal Films in 1978 and was also involved in the United Bamboo Gang mafia business in Taiwan. There was also the legal side: Because of a breach of contract, Jackie had to reckon with having to take legal action at any time.

Jackie was at the limit and asked Willie to help him, begging him to somehow get him out of this dubious contract. Willie finally made it with the help of the aforementioned Jimmy Wang Yu, to whom Jackie now owed two favours. Of course there were also judicial meetings, especially when Lo Wei brought a full-length film into the cinemas in 1983 with the *The Fearless Hyena 2* footage from 1979 with Jackie Chan in it. Against Jackie's will, of course.

During this time all hell was going on and it was often palpable and life-threatening on all sides. The whole chaos continued during the filming of *Dragon Lord*. Certain groups of people wanted to make it difficult for Jackie. They started fires on the set and put him under enormous psychological pressure. It is actually self-explanatory that Jackie Chan – now metaphorically speaking – was haunted by evil spirits.

All these negative feelings, the fear of an unknown future, the persecution of triad

Black Tavern from 1972. If you have the film at home, it is best to watch it again. Not only because it is one of the Shaws' lesser-known Wu Xia pearls – but also because a young Jackie Chan is apparently hiding here.

In addition to Mars, a young man plays one of official Hai's two servants and shares a few scenes in the snow until he… No spoilers at this point, just a thank you to Markus Popella for pointing this out. Looks hard like Jackie. So, if it looks like a Jackie, walks like a Jackie, and fights like a Jackie – then it's probably a Jackie.

But how does the ominous curse of Bruce Lee from the beginning fit in with an even more dubious curse of Jackie Chan? Even if he is not really superstitious himself, there were many producers and participants in the Hong Kong film landscape at the time. When Bruce Lee died in 1973, his office at Golden Harvest with almost everything in it was locked and only reopened when the new star Jackie Chan moved in right there in 1979. In Jackie's autobiography *Never Grow Up* he writes that there were even Bruce Lee's swords on a dresser.

members while he owed great gratitude to other gangsters and then the thematic confrontation with Chinese mythology and spirits over the years had to find an outlet at some point. And it stands to reason that that was the explanation for Jackie's ghost apparitions, which he hasn't mentioned since 1989.

Yes, even the rigidity of the body can be explained well, namely with the so-called sleep paralysis. This rigidity or temporary paralysis of the body during sleep is a natural protective mechanism so that the sleeper does not injure himself in violent movements at night. Subconsciously, Jackie had a bad trip going on.

Unfortunately, there is still no classic ghost film with him (*Rouge* is an exception for the drama genre, which he only produced). But we can be content with vampires in *The Twins Effect*, even if they are more Western and not Chinese Jiangshi. Or a short horror fight sequence in *My Lucky Stars*. Oh yes, as I said, there is also *Spiritual Kung Fu*. And also in *The Knight of Shadows* from 2019, this time child-friendly, mythological demons and ghosts are a big thing.

Visitation of ancient demons
Who knows what Jackie Chan really saw and whether the paranormal is something from the beyond or our subconscious. However, old myths can be used as an

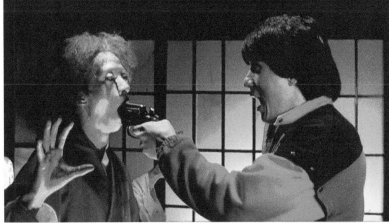

indication that people have always reacted subconsciously in one way or another and saw the same thing just like the woman in white. But next time you see a sick looking fellow hopping on the sidewalk, it is best to change the side of the street and take a day at the spa to appease your inner demons.

I wanted to come back to the jumping Yuen Wah from the Shaw production *The*

And it was only after he moved into this office that the turmoil began, including attempted murder, which he also describes in the same book. Has an evil demon lodged itself in Bruce Lee's office and haunted Jackie Chan? That would also be good material for a feature film that is reminiscent of classic sub-genres such as ghosts and ghosts-in-office films from Hong Kong in the 1980s. Imagine a lonely, busy Jackie Chan in such a horror scenario inside his secret hideout, where he lives and cuts films and… Oh, what could have been!

Jackie only suffered long-term damage in one form: He is still an omen when it comes to advertising for products that are no longer available a little later or that are involved in so called scandals. The best-known example would be the shampoo manufacturer Bawang, which was criticized for carcinogenic substances in its products. But that's another conspiracy theory.

In conclusion, there is only one thing left to say: ***Duang!***

Kickboxer from HELL

by Ken Miller

(1990)

Another production from the IFD film vaults to review! Woot!

Also known as ZODIAC POWER 3: KICKBOXER FROM HELL, this is a cut-and-paste IFD movie that intercuts new footage featuring western martial arts actor Mark Houghton with a 1976 Hong Kong/Korean supernatural movie called *The Obsessed*, starring Nora (*Way of the Dragon*) Miao.

The film begins with a woman called Sophia being chased by sackcloth-wearing bad guys. She stumbles upon a kickboxer called Sean (Houghton), who saves her. Back at Sean's home there is a funny conversation on the couch as Sophia explains things to Sean: "It's a long story – I'm a nun, actually – but my partner and I are working undercover against Lucifer." Excellent stuff! This explanation works as a tenuous link to the existing footage from *The Obsessed*: the newlywed heroine in this 1976 production, played by Nora Miao, is meant to be Sophia's partner, who has now given up being a nun and has married a stocky guy called Robert.

In this part of the plot we see creepy things start to happen, such as a broken clock starting to work again in the family home and a scene where Robert and his wife are given their wedding photos... and each shot features the ghostly face of his dead first wife Lisa. Creepy!

Back with the newly-shot footage, we cut to the dark HQ of the Lucifer-worshippers, who like to wear face paint and sackcloth. After some amusing trash-talk bickering (the dialogue in the new scenes is priceless), the two dudes who failed to catch Sophia are forced to fight to the death in a martial arts ring. One of the combatants dies when his groin is punched!

Jumping over to the haunted home yarn, we see a young maid encounter a 'guest' who is actually the ghost of first spouse Lisa. Lisa is always lit by green or blue lighting. At one point the slightly scabby-faced Lisa cackles as she eats some watermelon.

Back with the Sean plotline, the sackcloth Satanists capture Sophia as music stolen from *Halloween* plays on the soundtrack. The main Satanist henchman, who prefers to wear shades and a red bandana rather than sackcloth, kills Sean's brother! Before

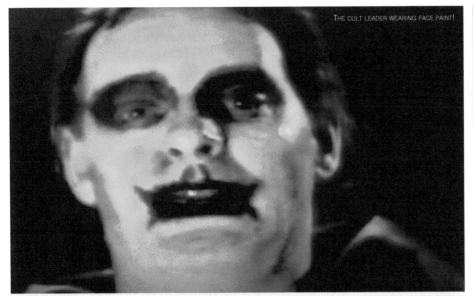

THE OBSESSED

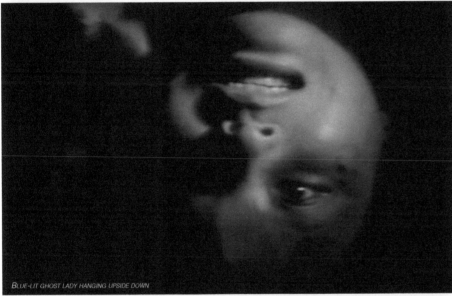

BLUE-LIT GHOST LADY HANGING UPSIDE DOWN

LISA SUDDENLY HAS VAMPIRE FANGS!

we can see how Sean reacts to this, we cut back to the ghost storyline. We see blue-lit ghostly Lisa brush her hair in a mirror and wonder whether the bent-over old housekeeper character is a nice or bad person.

The new wife is smothered by Lisa's floating wedding gown… or is the wife

imagining things? (Of course she isn't!) The wife is then attacked in the garden at night-time by Lisa, but hubby Robert still decides to go on a pre-planned business trip. What a caring guy!

Ah, here's the midpoint twist: Robert is a bit of a deceitful womaniser and he's gone to a hotel to meet his lover. Ghostly Lisa

shows up and throws Robert into the sea, but Robert just brushes off this supernatural encounter like it was nothing and meets-up with his mistress in his hotel room. What a hound!

As Robert's lover takes a bath… a floating blue-lit hand appears, then Lisa strangles the mistress and throws her from a balcony!

After we see the Lucifer worshippers perform a ceremony, burning a photograph of the wife, we see her become compelled to attack her nephew. Robert returns home soon after and is shown photos of his house taken by some real estate guys. Each shot shows Lisa's ghostly image, but Robert just blames the realtors for taking bad photographs!

Later, blue-lit Lisa watches Robert kiss his new wife, then there's a flashback of Lisa's funeral from a few years ago. In another scene there is some kind of seance/ceremony that takes place in the cemetery and the bent-over housekeeper starts speaking with Lisa's voice, claiming that Lisa was murdered. Yikes!

Robert goes fishing and thinks back to when he was married to Lisa, who we see accusing him of marrying her just for her

money. The flashback ends with Robert strangling Lisa.

Back with the Sean plot thread, he fights a sackcloth dude (who I'm sure I saw being killed at the start of the film). Wearing a red vest, Sean kicks ass and beats the Satanist. He then fights another Lucifer-lover: "I don't know what pain is, but you do!"

Meanwhile, the ghost story reaches the point where we see Lisa's grave being dug up and there's no body! After the old housekeeper is knifed to death by Robert, we see him go to the garden and dig up Lisa's corpse. But why? Nobody knows it's buried here, so why dig it back up? Anyway, Robert is soon taunted by Lisa's ghost, which now has fangs like a vampire. Robert is attacked by her and he is eventually captured by the authorities.

But what I want to know is this: why did Lisa's ghost initially taunt and attack the innocent new wife and Robert's mistress, rather than immediately target the murderous husband? I guess it will remain a mystery.

Now the Sean-vs-Satanists section of the film reaches its climax ("You'll pay for my brother!") as the hero confronts the Lucifer-worshipping bad guys at their HQ, where Sophia the young undercover nun is being held prisoner.

Sean and the main henchman fight each other with sledgehammers (as the theme from *Re-Animator* plays). The fight ends when Sean breaks the guy's neck. Sean now begins to break a series of skulls (that

each have a candle) because he realises this is the way to remove the Satanists' power.

The cult leader, who sports KISS-style face paint, brings the broken-necked main henchman back to life, but Sean dodges a swinging

sledgehammer blow and the final sacred skull gets smashed, causing the cult leader to die.

And then… we get an abrupt IFD-style finish: the end!

The scenes from *The Obsessed* are well enough done, with the story possessing a little bit of mystery, but not much effort is made by IFD this time to make this plot line seem at all relevant to the Satanists story.

The new footage with Houghton (who appeared in such Hong Kong actioners as *Tiger on the Beat 2*) is fun to watch, however, and I enjoyed listening to the sackcloth-wearing bad guys pettily swear amongst themselves. Some of the fighting was okay, too.

FANATICAL FD DRAGON

PRESENTS

5 FINGERS OF DISCS

by Johnny Burnett
aka Fanatical Dragon
www.youtube.com/FanaticalDragon

The last few months since issue 2 of Eastern Heroes, has seen a steady flow of some truly standout Blu-ray releases celebrating a selection of the very best slices of HK action and classic kung fu, and as we head steadily into the colder winter months, things are heating up even more! We have a one true Cat 3 heavyweight, A Jackie Chan classic we've all been holding out hope to see restored, finally getting it's release date, one incredible example of Wu Xia at its most inventive featuring a memorable encounter with 'multiple regular ninjas assembling into one giant ninja' likely the only one you'll ever see! Plus I have a sneak peek at what's absolutely going to be the very best Blu-Ray release of 2021 along with some long forgotten Shaw's classics imported from France. And if all that isn't enough to whet your kung fu loving appetites, I'm also very also proud to kickoff our first Eastern Heroes Blu-Ray competition in a collaboration with our good friends at 88 Films! Let's cram all 5 fingers full of discs once again dear readers! To start off strong, Let's wrap our own intestines around our opponents neck and get stuck right into...

Riki:Oh – The Story of Ricky Deluxe Edition
88 Films – (Region B)
1991. Director: Lam Ngai-kai
Out Now

A live action adaptation of the ultraviolent Manga of the same name, Riki:Oh is actually a far more charming and heartfelt movie than its jaw smashing, chest punching, eyeball popping action sequences would suggest. The story of our hero, imprisoned after taking bloody revenge against the gangsters who caused the death of his fiancé and winding up incarcerated in a privately run highly corrupt, super max prison proves a great vehicle for star Fan Sui-wong who gets to act onscreen alongside his father, Fan Mei-sheng, himself a former Shaw Brothers and Golden Harvest actor who gleefully rises to the occasion here as the hook handed

deputy warden hellbent on breaking our titular star. Ricky has to fight to protect his fellow inmates, fight to stop the various prison gangs from killing him, fight against the demented prison staff and ultimately, fight for his freedom!

Another in 88 Films ongoing wave of classic Cat 3 HK movies, and absolutely the best of the titles they've picked for this Category 3 series so far. The utterly insane and highly enjoyable *Riki:Oh – The Story of Ricky* crashed onto Blu-Ray in 88 Film's now familiar 'deluxe' edition format, bundled with a full rigid slipcase, as hard as Riki-oh's punches, a double sided poster, a meaty forty-page book and four lobby card reprints all wrapped up behind some gloriously OTT cover art courtesy of my own personal favourite cover artist, the incomparable Kung Fu Bob O'Brien.

88 have really pushed the boat out with extra features for this release, assembling

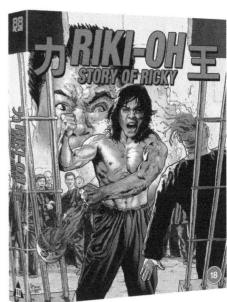

no less than four audio commentary tracks from 88 regulars – Arne Venema and *Eastern Heroes* frequent collaborator, Big Mike Leeder as well as a separate track from former Tai Seng Video producer, Asian Movie Expert and commentary maestro Frank Djeng.

Empire Magazine's Kim Newman records a track alongside Sean Hogan and we also get a fourth track from Video Games producers Audi Sorlie and Chris Ling. We also get archive interviews ported over from the old Hong Kong Legends DVD, most notably is a great interview with Ricky himself, Fan Sui-wong who talks at length at how controversial the movie was at the time for it's use of gore, the film did end up working against the young actor for a while and it would be some time before he would take the leading role in another movie again, working instead in supporting roles over the years (pretty consistently) he comes across as a very likeable and dedicated martial arts performer.

Audio options for the movie deliver both Cantonese and English dubs of the movie.

The Bastard Swordsman(1983 and Return of the Bastard Swordsman(1984)
Double Pack Blu-Ray Spectrum Films
Directed by Lu Chin-ku
Out Now

Norman Chui Siu-keung fans are well served recently, not only do they have the wonderful *Duel to the Death* release covered elsewhere in this very article, but Spectrum Films in France also recently released two standout double packs showcasing four absolutely fantastic slices of Shaw Brothers Wu Xia insanity, two of which also star Norman Chui.

Duel to the Death
Eureka Entertainment – (Region B)
1983. Director: Ching Siu-tung
Out Now

Eureka video recently put out Ching Siu-tung's debut feature film, the gleefully bonkers *Duel to the Death* from 1983, a classic Wu Xia tale with many added ninjas and showcasing some of the best FX and wire work to come out of HK in the '80s (and outclassing much of what we would see in the '90s).

This epic tale of a contest between the best Japanese and Chinese swordsman coming together for, as the title suggests, A Duel to the Death, gives us a damn good idea of the level of choreographic quality and inventiveness that Ching Siu-tung would later bring to *Hero*, *The House of Flying Daggers* and Tsui Hark's *Swordsman* series.

This is absolutely one of the best HK movies Eureka have put out to date, borderline essential viewing for any action movie fan. Where else can you see many small ninjas assembling into one giant super ninja 'Voltron style'?

Extras are a mix of old and new, archival interviews with stars Flora Cheung and Norman Chui Siu-keung ported over from the old Hong Kong Legends DVD along with a newly recorded (and insanely detail packed) commentary track by Frank Djeng along with Frank's original

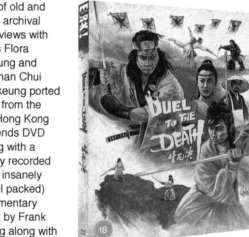

liner notes from the Tai Seng Laserdisc release. We also get a new interview created for the disc with screen writer Manfred Wong.

Eureka also present their customary booklet with writings from Eureka HK regular James Oliver (limited to 2,000 copies). Cover art is by Darren Wheeling and is really, really not to my taste, thankfully we get the original HK poster art as an alternate choice on the reversible sleeve, something very much lacking from Eureka's last big releases *Encounter of the Spooky Kind* and *Millionaire's Express*.

We get English and Cantonese audio options, both sound great and the quality of the print restoration on this, is absolutely first rate, the film has never looked better, almost too good in places, as the wires used to fly our key actors back and forth in combat are now very clearly visible, for me this just added to the movie. It's a glorious testament to some of the very best wire work that HK action cinema has ever presented whilst in its Golden age.

One of the most fun movies that Eureka has put out all year, and they've put out loads of classics.

The Bastard Swordsman and its sequel *Return of the Bastard Swordman* feature on the first double set, with truly breathtaking restoration scans. The films look so incredibly good on these Spectrum releases it's the main reason I like to include them here. There are no English Subtitles on their Blu-Rays, which maybe a stumbling block for some, but the quality of the release is truly exceptional.

It comes along at the same time as Spectrum have released another double feature, of two even more insane Wu Xia, fantasy martial arts spectaculars... namely...

The Chinese Boxer
88 Films
1970. Director: Wang Yu
Released 8th Dec 2021 (Region B, UK)
9th Dec 2021 (Region A, US)

88 films made a very welcome return to their numbered Asia Collection series earlier in November with their fantastic release of arguably Jimmy Wang Yu's best film, 1970's The Chinese Boxer. Taking over the helm as director on a movie which built on his success at Shaw Brothers leading from *The One Armed Swordsman*, *The Chinese Boxer* would cement (or iron palm) Wang Yu's status as one of the most significant actors and directors of the early '70s

88's release is a thing of beauty, glorious cover art by the mighty Kung Fu Bob O'Brien whose art graces not only the slipcover and case cover (reversible with the original HK poster art) but also on a limited edition poster (also with reversible

HK cover art) and on the disc itself.

The quality of the transfer of the movie itself is of the same jaw-dropping quality that I've come to expect from 88 films, the film has never looked better, colours and fantastically vibrant and there is no motion blur or HDR smoothing visible even during the film's climatic snow set final acts.

We get both English and Cantonese audio options as is somewhat standard now for the label along with a commentary track by film critic Samm Deighan (returning to the label again after her detail laden track on *Come Drink With Me*). We also get a Frédéric Ambroisine archive interview with Wong Ching and a solid 17 min featurette from David West covering the impact of the movie and its effect on the HK movies that followed. TV spots and trailers round out the single disc release.

This release represents 88's first foray into dual territory releasing for their Shaws titles, coming out both in the UK and also now the US, hopefully this will allow the company to thrive even more and to expand their release schedule into more and more Shaws titles in 2022.

Holy Flame of The Martial World (1983) and The Demon of The Lute (1983)
Double Pack Blu-Ray Spectrum Films
Directed by Lu Chin-ku
and Tang Tak-cheung
Out Now

The Demon of the Lute is really designed as a kids film, announcing itself as much in the opening dedication to the world's children, but don't let that put you off tracking down what is one of the best examples of '80s Shaw Brothers martial arts excess.

I think if it as a more colourful and slightly more fun companion to the type of OTT action which *Duel to the Death* (and to a certain extent *Story of Ricky*) also embodies.

Jam packed with Shaw's regulars, with Kara Hui, Chin Siu-ho, Yuen Tak and Philip Kwok leading the charge against Chen Kwan Tai's villain (decked out for much of the film in a Darth Vader inspired black helmet). Realism takes a back seat to hyperactive action and super powered fighters, being well… super.

Overall it's an outlandish and densely layered tale of martial arts secret weapons and world domination plots, good stuff.

Demon of the Lute is bundled alongside *Holy Flame of The Martial Arts*, another laser packed, wire work totting, FX extravaganza that just like *DOTL* won't be to everyone's tastes, but for me showcases the more light hearted and fun side of Shaws, somewhat of a final act for these types of movie from SB as a dark cloud would descend over the studio the following year with the untimely death of Alexander Fu Sheng and the beginning of the end for motion picture production at Clearwater bay. It's nice to have these two colourful trophies from the studio together on one set looking so good. And the Spectrum releases look DAMN good.

All the Spectrum movies have only French subtitles with original Cantonese audio.

Shawscope Vol 1 Boxset

Arrow Video – 12 movies, 2 audio CDs
Directors: Chang Cheh, Lau Kar-leung
Available now
Released 13th Dec 2021 (Region B, UK)
14th Dec 2021 (Region A, US)

I was lucky enough to get my Buddhist fists on the review discs for Arrow Video's first foray into the wonderful world of Shaw Brothers movies, and what a debut it has turned out to be. This twelve movie boxset arrives with an almighty kick to the head of the competition, thanks in part due to Arrow's already spectacular reputation for delivering top notch restorations of classic Japanese Cinema and their ability to put together a well crafted and intelligently thought out package of extras. The set ups-the-ante in all regards.

Seven of the twelve movies have completely new restorations created by Arrow for the set, almost all the extra features across the dozen films have never been seen before or have been crafted specifically for the box set and are of Criterion levels of quality (going so far as to heavily feature the insanely knowledgable Tony Rayns, who contributes often to Criterion's East Asian cinema releases). The set is a careful curated mix of classic Shaw's kung fu with one notable exception, their choice of *Mighty Peking Man* may seem strange, as it's the sole title in the set which already had a UK Blu-Ray release a few years ago, thanks to 88 films, however, as Arrow have been making more and more strides into releasing their titles in the USA and as *The Mighty Peking Man* is a Quentin Tarantino favourite, I suspect this has been a calculated choice designed to draw in the Kalju and Monster movie fans who all salivated over Arrow's *Gamera*, *Daimajin* and recently, their Yokai Monsters boxsets.

All of the other eleven movies presented here have never had Blu-Ray releases in the UK, and only *Five Deadly Venoms* had a US release via Dragon Dynasty which was an upscale from DVD and pales in

comparison to the quality of the restoration on show here.

The set is dominated by the work of two of Shaw's most celebrated directors, Chang Cheh and (his one time fight choreographer) Lau Kar-leung both feature most heavily with six and four movies each respectively. The full list of titles included here are *King Boxer*, *The Boxer from Shantung*, *Shaolin Temple*, *5 Shaolin Masters*, *The Mighty Peking Man*, *Challenge of the Masters*, *Executioners from Shaolin*, *The Chinatown Kid*, *The 5 Deadly Venoms*, *Crippled Avengers*, *Heroes of the East* and *Dirty Ho*.

This set easily takes the trophy for the best release of 2021 for me, it's hard to imagine Arrow doing any better than they have with the boxset, from the quality of the

remasters, the bundled extras right down to the menu artwork commissioned for each film, the quality across the board is impeccable. Commentary tracks lean more towards the academic, but manage to stay on the right side of being fun and engaging rather than feeling like a college lecture.

The variety of interviews from Frédéric Ambroisine's archives are all fascinating and the hours of newly created content featuring Tony Rayns is worth the price of the set on its own. We also get a welcome return of the old *Cinema Hong Kong* Documentary from 2003, running at just over fifty mins and interviewing almost every HK star of note along with some great behind the scenes footage of Lau Kar-leung on the set of *Drunken Monkey*.

As if the movies and their extras weren't enough, Arrow have also produced two full audio CDs of music from the De Wolfe music library, all presented here sounding better than I've ever heard them before, both run for close to an hour. and include full music tracks along with some classic audio 'stings' from the movies featured in the set.

If you only pickup one boxset this winter season, I'd highly recommend you make it this one. Highly, highly recommended.

COMPETITION TIME!!
Dragons Forever 88 Films Limited Edition Steelbook

I'm delighted to be able to announce our first Eastern Heroes giveaway since the magazine relaunch earlier this year, We have one glorious brand spanking new *Dragons Forever* Steelbook courtesy of our friends over at 88 Films, these were limited to 2,000 copies only, feature glorious cover art by Thomas Walker and include a full slipcase and poster. Jam packed with extra features the 88 films release of this Jackie, Sammo and Yuen Biao Classic is the most definitive version of the last on screen outing of these three legends anywhere worldwide!

To be in with a chance of winning this fantastic Steelbook, all you have to do to enter is simply snap a selfie of yourself holding this month's issue of the magazine and e-mail it to us over at: **easternheroescompetition@gmail.com**

A winner will be picked on the Monday 3rd January 2022 to give all of our American friends a chance to get their hands on this issue and be able to also enter. I'll be announcing the winner over on my YouTube channel, so do please subscribe to the channel, and Eagle Claw that bell for notifications to stay updated when new videos are posted... just search for 'The Fanatical Dragon' on YouTube and you'll find me there. *Good Luck to all who enter!*

Armour of God Deluxe Edition
88 Films – (Region B)
1986. Director: Jackie Chan
Available 27th December 2021
Limited Edition 2 x Blu-ray Disc set

Just in time to see out 2021 with a dynamite bang, 88 films are all set to release a Deluxe edition of the movie that very nearly killed Jackie Chan... the stunt laden classic *Armour of God*!

We get to see the first time Jackie portrayed his Asian Hawk character on screen, in this globe trotting action adventure classic, absolutely bursting with some truly exceptional stunts and martial arts battles.

88 Are pulling out all the stops and giving this one the Deluxe treatment and making it their most loaded JC release yet, we're set to get our mitts on a full rigid slipcase with another stunning slice of cover art by the Sharpie Samurai himself, Kung Fu Bob O'Brien.

Six replica lobby cards and a double sided poster accompany a eighty-eight page bound book stacked with essays and archive materials.

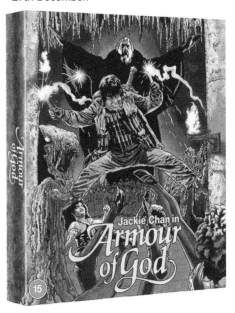

On the two discs themselves we get a mountain of extras including three commentary tracks, two different cuts of the movie, including a newly restored 4K scan from the original negative, another vintage episode of the great *Celebrity Talk Show* TV show from HK (subtitled) which 88 also managed to secure another episode of for their release of *Erotic Ghost Story*. This show is truly a great slice of HK history and I for one can't wait to see Jackie Chan on the show talking *Armour Of God*! We also get an episode of Scott Adkins excellent original show *The Art of Action* with Scott being joined by Matt Routledge to talk all things JC. And lots, lots more!

The set will be released in the UK on the 27th December.

www.88films.co.uk